Phil & Lynn
Partners in ministry
Sharers of dreams
Makers of music

EASY
DOESN'T
Do It

& especially friends.

Dennis

CONTENTS

Foreword

Derric Johnson Communicates! What he writes touches the head and the heart. It is both simple and profound. He has that unique capacity of taking everyday events and drawing from them eternal implications.

I've known him for twenty years now and have counted him as a friend as well as a fellow minister. He served on the staff of this Church for three years and was always a source of creativity, motivation and inspirational good will to all of us.

Derric uses words like a surgeon uses a scalpel. These writings will make some sharp incisions into your soul, but the purpose of the temporary pain is to bring wholeness and healing. Like surgery, you will be much healthier after the process.

These essays will also paint pictures of the possibilities of people who are truly committed to God's will. You will catch yourself remembering those illustrations and applying the principles in specific situations. Derric's positive word pictures have a way of becoming permanent in a person's memory.

These inspirational essays point out the essential truths of life. Most of us read them and wonder, "Why didn't I think of that?" He has that gift that makes us think about things that we haven't thought of before.

You will be informed, amused, convicted, stretched, and motivated by these essays. I'll warn you early that you'll learn more than you expect. Each essay has a hook . . . and it will usually get you when you are least expecting. But you will be a better person for it!

Read each one with an open mind . . . and an open heart. You can't remain the same. Be truly open to all that God wants to communicate to you through these assertations. You will struggle some . . . but you will grow. After all, easy doesn't do it!

John Ed Mathison
Senior Minister
Frazer Memorial United Methodist Church
Montgomery, Alabama

A Church Conference was in progress at Azusa Pacific University. A young man sought me out asking for an opportunity to visit. He was concerned for his ministerial future since he had approached three different denominations and no openings were available. "No one seems to need me," were his apprehensive words.

After considerable conversation we realized <u>we needed each other</u>. Our hearts were knit together in faith to lead an unwieldy new congregation of mostly unsaved people to become a part of the body of Christ. We dreamed together, planned together, sacrificed together and prayed together for thirteen years.

Other staff was added and contributed much, but Derric Johnson deserves a great deal of credit for the growth and spiritual development of Skyline Wesleyan Church in Lemon Grove, California.

His indefatigable energy, innovative planning and inspirational spirit along with compelling charm presents a multi-talented person -- preacher, teacher, mentor and musician.

Read <u>EASY DOESN'T DO IT</u> and experience a fresh insight into the practicality of living an energized life in Christ from a man who is in God's school of learning.

Orval Butcher
Pastor Emeritus
Skyline Wesleyan Church
Lemon Grove, California

INTRODUCTION

When one of my colleagues heard that I was writing a book, he asked, "How long does that take?"

The answer, of course, is very simple. "For me . . . about thirty years!"

At least that's how long I've been gathering material,

sorting clippings,

fabricating illustrations,

sharing anecdotes,

culling axioms,

tracing cliches,

enjoying maxims,

forming mottos,

studying proverbs,

incorporating quips,

and citing quotes.

This material has been used in thousands of services, seminars and ceremonies across the country. If you can find continued value in these ideas . . . they're yours to share.

To all my friends who encouraged me to do this,
to all the cohorts who wanted copies and clippings,
to my wife, Debbie, who dared me to risk it,
to all the cynics who said I couldn't,
I wouldn't,
I shouldn't,
. . . this is for you.

Never say IMPOSSIBLE to a believer. That will be his
goad to the goal . . . because easy doesn't do it!
Never has! Still doesn't! Never will!

To Dr. Orval C. Butcher, Pastor Emiritus,
Skyline Wesleyan Church,
Lemon Grove, California
and Dr. John Ed Mathison, Senior Minister,
Frazer Memorial United Methodist Church,
Montgomery Alabama
my two main ministry friends from whom I learned
with whom I shared
and to whom I owe so much,
thanks for the words of introduction to this collection.

Lee Ann Martin provided invaluable assistance and creativity in the artwork and typesetting. One word for her. . .
peerless.

And to Jerry and Jackie Evans . . . my everlasting gratitude
for going the second mile. It's been a great journey.

DERRIC JOHNSON
Orlando, Florida

1

WOULD YOU KNOW ONE IF YOU SAW ONE?

The local business man was teaching a Sunday School Class of fourth-grade boys. He especially wanted to be impressive because his son was a member of The Class.

During the lesson he asked, "Now why do you suppose that people call me a Christian?"

The query was met with stoney silence . . . so he asked again, "Why do you suppose that people call me a Christian?"

Still no response. Mr. Arthur paused . . . scratched his chin . . . and repeated his question, "Come on now. Think. Why do people call me a Christian?"

Out of the silence his son spoke up, "Maybe they don't know you!"

"What is a Christian?" Always a fair topic for discussion. Suppose we rephrase it: **"WOULD YOU KNOW ONE IF YOU SAW ONE?"**

The early followers of Jesus never called themselves Christians, you know. That title, appearing 3 times in the New Testament, is always offered by the secular world. It was applied at first in derision . . . and later in respect.

Those "little Christs" chose to call themselves other names:

SAINTS . . . bespeaking their spiritual health and holiness,
BELIEVERS . . . denoting their faith,
DISCIPLES . . . pointing out their learning and discipline,
BROTHERS and SISTERS . . . referring to their fellowship.

And how those spiritual pilgrims loved to be together. Actually, "togetherness" was their most cherished and meaningful situation. In fact the word "saint" meaning one who is God's very own, appears 99 times in the New Testament . . . and it is always plural. Every time it is saints . . . you can't have just one. A saint ain't! Saints come in twos.

Just as coals in a fire need the warmth of other embers, or they grow cold and die, we need the fellowship of each other to keep the fire cooking.

The tallest tree is always in the middle of the forest . . . That's because strength comes from association with friends.

When Paul writes to the Hebrews "Not forsaking the assembling of ourselves together . . . but exhorting one another" he really is underlining the purpose of our gathering. The word "exhorting" in the original language carries the thought of "encouraging".

Now, that's a switch! I always thought I should go to Church to get what I needed. Instead . . . I'm supposed to be giving other people what they need. (Do you think that that's what Jesus really meant when He said, "Do unto others as you would have them do unto you"?)

If I need love . . . I should give love,
not look for it as a gift from others.

If I need enthusiasm . . . I ought to
offer it to someone else who needs it.

If I'm lonely and just wish someone would
smile at me . . . I guess I should find
someone to grin at.

So it seems safe to say that the focus of fellowship is not "what's in it for me" . . . but "what's in me for it".

An ambitious farmer, unhappy about the yield of his crops, heard of a highly recommended new seed corn. He bought some and produced a crop that was so abundant, his astonished neighbors asked him to sell them a portion of his new seed. But the farmer refused. After all, why should he lose his profitable and competitive advantage?

The second year his new seed did not produce as good a crop, and when the third-year crop was still worse, it dawned on the farmer that his prize corn was being pollinated by the inferior grade of corn from the fields of his neighbors whom he had refused to help!

You know that the giant redwood trees grow only on the West Coast of America. No place else on this earth. Those mammoth trees have always been favorites of mine. Ever since Mom and Pop took us on annual family vacations there, I have been drawn back again and again, thrilled and awed just to stand in their shadow.

Debbie and I drove out of the way and picnicked in one of those groves on a recent Saturday, while travelling between Sacramento and San Francisco. The strength and size of those trees are stunning. They are giants . . . standing so close together that their branches seem to filter the sun right out of the day, and their towering tops brush the clouds from the sky.

If that seems too poetic . . . go stand there yourself. The majesty of it all demands talk in whispers between the long moments of silent staring. And in your heart you keep repeating, "Only God . . ."

Most of the trees have burn and char scars, recalling difficulties past. Some even have huge caverns carved out of their middles by gutting fires . . . so big that two or three people can stand inside . . . but they still grow, so full of life they can't be killed. And that makes all the scars seem unimportant.

We wandered over to the tree that Colonel Armstrong discovered. It towered 308 feet over us. That's more than 30 stories tall! It's been alive 1,400 years, which means that when Columbus discovered America, that tree was already 900 years old.

It's as if one day God said, "I think I'll build a tree. Who cares if it takes 500 years or a thousand or whatever. I just want a tree. Who's counting?"

Don't you suppose that He has some of the same patience with your growth? Character takes time . . . and scars. But God keeps going for the ultimate and that's part of what He meant when He said, "And he shall be like a tree."

So what's the secret of the redwood? How can it last so long and endure so much?

Unlike the palm tree whose tap root goes down into the ground as deep as the tree is tall (30 feet up . . . 30 feet down), the redwood has no tap root at all. That's why you never see a redwood standing alone. Never. They are always in clusters . . . groups . . . groves.

The might of the tree is not in itself. Here is its strength . . . for every foot in height . . . the redwood tree sends its roots, not down, but three times that distance . . . **OUT!**

That's right . . . **OUT!** If the tree is 300 feet tall, its roots go 900 feet out . . . intertwisting with all the groping roots from the other redwoods in the grove. By the time a few thousand years go by, those fellowshipping roots are so woven with one another, there is no way a tree could fall down. It is held up by the strength of its brothers and sisters.

So how long will you grow? How tall will you be? What trials will be yours?

Who's counting? I just heard God say, *"I think I'll build a tree . . . and he shall not stand alone."*

2

THAT WAS MY IDEA

Isn't it interesting that before a person becomes a believer everything that goes wrong is blamed on God? Then after we become part of the Church, everything bad is an attack of Satan. Somehow, it's never me who makes a mistake. Everything bad is someone else's fault.

During a fierce summer storm, our reinforcing wall collapsed, sending piles of mud and gallons of dirty water into our brand new swimming pool. I called Marge, our insurance agent to report the disaster.

"Welcome to the club," was her cheerful reply. "That was the heaviest rain for an eight hour period in 50 years. You're the seventeenth person to call this morning. Walls are down all over town!"

"Marge," I replied, "that information hardly brings comfort to my mind. It's like calling my dentist and telling him I have a toothache, and hearing him say, 'Don't worry, I have one, too.' I want to know what you're going to do about my wall and my pool!"

"Let me check to see if you have flood insurance," she dodged.

"Flood insurance?" I couldn't believe my ears. "Marge, we live on the highest elevation in this county. If it ever floods up here, your office would be in no condition to pay my claim. Why would I ever buy flood insurance?"

"Let me check anyway," she said as she punched the hold button, sending me into telephonic oblivion.

Back on the line she muttered, "No luck. Your falling wall is classified as an ACT OF GOD."

"Are you kidding me? Surely, your Company believes that God has more important things to do than run around in the rain, knocking down walls."

"Sorry," was the last sound I heard as she rushed on to answer her next call.

I knew it wouldn't do any good, but I just couldn't resist calling her back thirty minutes later. "Guess what! I just talked to God! He says He didn't do it!"

(Neither did the other guy.)

The blame really needs to be fixed on a building contractor who saved a few bucks by not putting enough support for the wall into the hill. It was easy enough to fix once we figured out who was at fault.

When my brother was still young enough to always tell the truth (interesting how we learn to shade it as we "mature") he was involved in a neighborhood ruckus. Ron was sitting on top of a kid, hitting him with both fists as hard as any 4 year-old could. Mom stopped the fight by pinning both Ron's arms behind his back.

But you know little brothers. He wasn't through yet . . . so he bent over and bit the other kid on the nose.

Over the squeals of anguish, Mom said firmly, "Ron! Stop right now! Satan must have made you do that!"

Ron's honest reply: "Maybe Satan made me hit him, but biting his nose . . . that was MY idea."

"My idea!" You do get a vote in this life, you know. Attitudes are yours to make.

I was walking with a friend in New York City, when he stopped for a newspaper and said, "Good morning."
The vendor grouched back, "What's good about it?"
"Well, for one thing, it's a new day," continued my friend, "and we're still alive."
"Not for long," was the retort. "You haven't read the paper yet."
"But I bet I find something good when I do," he said, flipping a quarter onto the counter.
"Boy, is he in a lousy mood this morning," was my astute observation.
"He's always that way . . . every morning," my friend confided.
"Then why are you so nice to him?"
"Why should I let him decide how I'm going to act?" was the conversation stopper.
Attitudes . . . your idea.
Like the third grader who had to wear glasses because of deficient eye sight. His aunt saw him for the first time with his "four eyes" and exclaimed with sympathy, "How terrible for a 9-year old to have to wear those things."
"Oh, glasses aren't so bad in the third grade. The guys won't hit you . . . and the girls won't kiss you!"
And that attitude . . . that's his idea.

We have a best friend in Orlando who is a Doctor. More specifically, a Gastroenterologist . . . that means he spends most of his time working on the lower insides of people. Consequently, many of his patients are elderly. After thoroughly checking one lady who was 102 years old, he said, "You're in remarkably good shape. I hope I get to see you again."

"Oh, I'll see you next year," was her quick reply.

"You sound pretty confident of that," the Doctor mused.

"Why, I certainly am. Don't you know the statistics? Not many people die between 102 and 103."

Her attitude . . . her choice.

Got time for one more? A little boy fell on the playground at school and cut his head.

Three stitches.

One hour later he butted heads with a girl and knocked out two of his teeth.

At lunch he tripped and sprained his wrist.

The school principal took him home before another disaster could occur and on the drive, noticed the boy's clenched fist. When she asked what he was holding, the little boy said, "A quarter. I found it on the playground when I got knocked down and I've been holding it ever since. I never found a quarter before. This is the luckiest day of my life!"

MAKE IT WHAT YOU CHOOSE

The artist had finished his painting,
The last of his brush strokes was done;
He paused to look at his picture
Of the mountain and valley and sun.

A stranger came by and he studied
The canvas with deep furrowed brow.
"The beauty I understand clearly,
It's the meaning I need to know now.

The sun is half-hidden by mountains,
It looks dark in the valley to me;
Is it early or late? The dawn or the dusk?
Is it sunrise or sunset I see?"

The artist paused . . . then explained,
The difference there was in the views;
"Sunrise or sunset? Day's dawn or day's gone?
You can make it whatever you choose!"

Remember Joshua's advice? "Choose you this day . . ."
Make it the best ever.
Your choice . . . your idea.

3

JUST A WORD . . . OR SO

$\mathbf{A}$ friend says you should know this:

The six most important words . . .
> I ADMIT I MADE A MISTAKE.

The five most important words . . . . .
> YOU DID A GOOD JOB.

The four most important words . . . .
> WHAT IS YOUR OPINION?

The three most important words . . . .
> I AM SORRY.

The two most important words . . . .
> THANK YOU.

The least important of all . . . . I.

But somehow most of us have twisted the emphasis and made the "I" word incredibly important. In fact English is the only major language in the world that capitalizes the first person singular pronoun.

We share a 13 year old, Stephanie, in our house, and like every young teen, she spends a lot of time and energy on first person emphasis.

"I want . . ."
"I have to . . ."
"I wish . . ."
"I won't . . ."

So to increase our awareness of that propensity, which does appear from time to time in every family member (except Mommy) we have a game we play . . . especially on long trips.

Each person in the car gets a vial of dimes (25 of them will fit in a small container available from your pharmacist). Any time anyone uses the word **I, ME, MY, or MINE** . . . that person forfeits one dime to the person who first hears it and then claims it.

This, of course, is designed to get all of us to think creatively before we speak. Rather than say,

**"I WANT TO STOP!
I NEED TO GO TO THE BATHROOM."**

It is far better, considering the dime collection, to say,

**"SURELY SOMEONE WOULD
LIKE TO PULL OFF
AT THE NEXT REST STOP FOR SOME RELIEF!"**

Above all the weeping, wailing and gnashing of teeth at the loss of some silver . . . and the equally noisy squeals of glee at the addition to personal fortune, we really are learning to fine-tune the focus of our speech.

Then a few months ago, Stephanie whispered in my ear, "Let's skip Church this week and go home after Sunday School. Brother Jim's not preaching today (that's our Pastor) and the man who is, isn't very good!"

I asked why she felt that way and she said, "Because he talks about himself all the time."

"So, let's play our game. We have $100.00 for the offering this morning. Every time he says, **"I, ME, MY or MINE**, we'll take a dollar away."

"Neat idea!" was her reply. And guess what? We heard at one point these words:

> *"In my research, I have discovered a new meaning for this verse. I am anxious to share it this morning and I want you to listen carefully to my voice."*

Did you get that? In just two sentences, FIVE references to the pronoun referring to the first person. We all knew that Brother Jim would have said something like:

> *"There's a new meaning to this verse that we all should understand and take to heart."*

Same meaning . . . with no reference to **I, ME, MY, or MINE.**

Anyway . . . just 23 minutes into his sermon, our preacher logged his 100th first person pronoun . . . and we were on our way to a really good Sunday dinner.

(Don't worry . . . we did give the $100.00 to another ministry . . . but the lesson was deeply etched in our hearts.)

And you know . . . it even shows up in our music, often and strangely in what we call Worship and Praise Songs:

> I will rejoice,
> I will rejoice,
> I will rejoice and be glad in Him.

We outscore Him three to one there!

> He has made me glad,
> He has made me glad,
> I will rejoice for He has made me glad.

If you care, there's still more of us than Him.

Watch the focus . . . that's all.

If it is true that "out of the abundance of the heart, the mouth speaketh," then take care that your tongue doesn't cut your throat.

> Oh be careful little mouth what you say,
> Oh be careful little mouth what you say,
> For the Father up above
> Is looking down in love.
> So be careful little mouth what you say
> (and what you sing).

Here's to a little "i" and a great GOD.

4

HAPPY NEW YOU!

I love January first . . . it offers a brand new beginning.

It's an unspoiled book of blank pages,
   an uncharted sea,
    an untraveled road,
     an untrod path,
      an untasted feast,
       an unopened flower,
        an unknown symphony,
         an undrawn picture,
          an unseen benefit,
           an unused dream.

  Wouldn't it be great if just this one year, everything happened right on schedule and exactly according to your master plan. Or would it? Sometimes the unexpected is the greater experience. It's surprise and discovery and hope!

  Charles Goodyear failed in hundreds of experiments trying to improve the quality of rubber from cracking-cold in winter and decomposing-hot in summer. On the edge of quitting, he accidently spilled some of his sticky substance on a hot stove, discovered vulcanization and gave us the rubber industry.

Clarence was ice fishing in Minnesota and the fish he caught was quick-frozen in the minus 20 degree air but revived later in a bucket of water. Clarence investigated his accidental miracle, found that such quick freezing did not impair the cell structure of the fish and that gave birth to the frozen food industry and the company that bears his name. Clarence . . . Birdseye.

In 1787 a 26 year old Yankee clockmaker almost lost his job because he couldn't wake up at 4 A.M. to get to work on time. His "emergency" prompted the invention of the alarm clock. He never patented his device. His only reward? "I was never late again."

Ebenezer was forced from his nightly joy of newspaper reading by his wife's loud and constant complaining about the difficulties of sewing without patterns. He invented paper patterns and called them by his name. Ebenezer . . . Butterick.

These men found the secret of surviving their surprises. They wrapped beauty around trouble and gave us pearls.

Starting out this year . . . clean out the refrigerator. There is no room for leftovers. The Apostle Paul wrote strong words, "Forgetting the things which are behind . . . press on toward the mark of the high calling of God through Jesus Christ, our Lord."

What are your remnants of last year?
> Failures?
>> Successes?
>>> Mistakes?
>>>> Triumphs?
>>>>> Anger?
>>>>>> Victories?
>>>>>>> Anxieties?
>>>>>>>> Animosities?

Forget them all . . . good or bad!
> happy or sad!
>> sorry or glad!

And move forward . . . fast! Choose a target, pick a goal, proceed with a purpose. You heard about the sharpshooter in the hills of Tennessee? A reporter was dispatched from the Nashville *BANNER* to interview what had to be the best gunman of the century.

The newspaperman got to the village and was amazed to find targets everywhere . . . on barns, poles, trees . . . even the side of the town church. And dead in the center of each circled target was a single bullet hole. Perfect shot every time.

He asked at the General Store where to find this gun-totin' hero, and after a little chat and chew, the locals pointed him west of town. Said his name was "Lester, and be careful of stray bullets. He's shootin' all the time!"

The writer followed the sound of the bang-bangs and soon was face to face with a wild looking hill-man. "You're some kind of shot!"

"Yep," came the monosyllabic reply.

"Never miss, do you?"

"Nope."

The newsman went on, "One shot, dead center in every target! Amazing! I'd like to write a story about you. Mind telling me how you do it?"

"It's easy," came the modest reply. "I shoot first . . . and draw the circles later!"

But that only works in some make-believe area far away from real life. We need "circles first" in the here-and-now where we live today.

If it's true that a resolution is a promise made with purpose . . . then here are six worth committing to.

1. I will at least once a week commit myself to do something I don't want to do. It's good discipline and stretches my spiritual vitality.

2. I will invest my life in something that will outlast me.

3. I will ask less often this year, "What's in it for me?" and ask more often, "What's in me for it?"

4. I will remember that the best things in life aren't things.

5. I will enjoy the little things. Because some day I may look back and realize that they were the big things.

6. I will every day commit myself to be the person God wants me to be.

And good resolutions are like babies crying in Church.
They need to be carried out immediately. Don't wait around.
No time like now to start.

It is true that the present has been colored by the past.
It is also true that we choose the colors of the future.

To understand the mind of a person,
    look at what he has already achieved.
To understand the heart of a person,
    look at what he aspires yet to do.

I said to the man who stood at the gate of the year,
        "Give me a light
           that I may tread safely
       into the unknown."
And he replied,
        "Go out into the darkness
         and put your hand into the hand of God.
      That shall be to you better than light
     and safer than any known way."

I asked Debbie, our home's Mistress of Culinary Delight,
to come up with her recipe for a Great New Year. She said,

*Take twelve fine, full-grown months. Be sure that they are
thoroughly free from all old memories of bitterness, rancor, hate
and jealousy.*
Cleanse them completely from every clinging spite.
Pick off all specks of pettiness.
*Cut these months into thirty equal parts. This batch will keep
for just one year. Do not attempt to make up the whole batch at*

one time, but prepare one day at a time as follows:
Into each day put twelve parts of faith,
  eleven of patience,
    ten of courage,
      nine of work,
        eight of hope,
          seven of fidelity,
            six of liberality,
              five of kindness,
                four of rest,
                  three of prayer,
                    two of meditation,
                      one well selected resolution.

Add a teaspoonful of good spirits,
  a dash of fun,
    a sprinkling of play,
      a heaping cupful of good humor.

Pour love into all this and mix with vim.
Cook thoroughly in fervent heat.
Garnish with a few smiles
and a sprig of joy.

Then serve with quietness,
  unselfishness,
    and cheerfulness,
      and a Happy New Year is a certainty.

DURING THIS NEW YEAR MAY YOU HAVE:

Enough happiness to keep you sweet.
Enough distress to keep you strong.
Enough sorrow to keep you human.
Enough hope to keep you happy.
Enough determination to make today better than yesterday.
Enough failure to keep you humble.
Enough success to keep you eager.
Enough friends to give you comfort.
Enough wealth to meet your needs.
Enough enthusiasm to take you to tomorrow.
Enough commitment to be sure you have a

HAPPY NEW YOU.

5

I DON'T BELIEVE IN GOD!

The sharp looking, deep thinking, sensitive young man was sitting limply, staring at the wall. Reeling from his recent disappointments and failures he blurted out, "I just don't believe in God!" That statement was undoubtedly designed to send me shivering to the floor beneath my desk in fear and shock.

But I've learned (through no small bit of experience) that a specific definition here is valid. Rather than leap into the conversation with some "deep discussion of the ontological and teleological proofs of the existence of God, whether Deistic or Personal," the best thing to do is to ask a question back.

So I looked him right in the eye and said, "Please . . . tell me what kind of God you don't believe in. I probably don't believe in that one either."

Where did we pick up all our pictures of God? You know, the cosmic kill-joy who leans out over the balcony of heaven acting like a window-tapper at the drive-in movie saying, "Ah, ah, ah . . . don't do that!"

Or the God with the heavenly housing shortage . . . desperately finding ways to keep us OUT of His kingdom. "One false move and you're banished to "youknowwhere".

Or the vindictive little God who gets his joybells rung by getting even with us for all the bad things we do. "You do that again and I'm gonna gitcha!"

Or the omnipotent bellhop who tends to our every wish. We hand Him a to-do schedule every morning (calling it a prayer list) and then check in at night and rate Him on how well He did.

Well, none of those "gods" fill the bill. You don't believe in that kind of God? Neither do I.

Most of my misinformation about the Father came from my second grade Sunday School teacher. (Someday I'm going to write a book to expose her foggy theology).

It was she who taught me that if I was a good little boy, God would love me and smile on my life.

But if I acted or spoke or thought badly, then He couldn't love me any more or even help me. (Talk about conditional love!)

She launched the whole class on incredible guilt trips . . . like she'd made me feel that if I forgot to offer a prayer of thanks for my food . . . I could count on all sorts of sickness and pestilence, not to mention trips to the doctor and increased health insurance premiums for my Mom and Dad.
But if I'd bite the bullet of persecution in public, bow my head and remember "God", then my chances for good health and long life were greatly increased. (After some long discussion, it was agreed that I could pray with one eye open to protect my desserts from my little brother's wandering hand which seemed

to steal anything edible. While we "holy people" prayed to bless the food, he was stuffing his face with it.)

And her choice of Sunday School songs was always a concern of mine. Her favorite was "Jesus Wants Me for a Sunbeam". Do you remember that song? Did you like it? Boy, not me. I hated that ditty. It made no sense to me at all. A sunbeam! I didn't want to be a sunbeam. I was in the second grade . . . I wanted to be a cowboy or a fireman.

One day I asked my Mom what exactly was a sunbeam. She took an old pillow and walked it over to the window. It was late in the afternoon and the sun's rays were shining sideways through the venetian blinds. Mom popped the pillow with her hand and all this stuff floated into the air. She said in her voice of awe, "Those . . . are . . . sunbeams."

Well ! ! !

Then I was sure I didn't want to be a sunbeam. Floating aimlessly through the air. Forget it!

You see, to that second grade Sunday School teacher, being a sunbeam for Jesus meant sitting quietly, feet on the floor, hands folded in lap, watching intently (with both eyes) as she taught her flann-o-graph lesson. This was God's perfect will for my life.

I have news for you. God doesn't want sunbeams! Not you. Not me. He doesn't need docile people to float through life. He's looking for revolutionaries who will change this world with the Gospel.

So what kind of a God can we believe in? What is He really like? How do we trust Him? And how do we get to know Him?

First of all He is a God of Love. No . . . more than that. He is Love. Some people say that you can't know anything about love unless you know Him. But I think the more you know about love . . . the more you know about God. So care . . . and share . . . and dare to love. Not for you . . . but for Him.

And He's a God of Light
> Life
>> Justice
>>> Holiness.

> He is the author and finisher of faith
> the first and the last
> the everlasting father
> the wonderful counselor
> the prince of peace
and the source of all joy and satisfaction.

My Mom must have been the originator of the phrase, "Try it . . . you'll like it." She could do more exotic things to disguise green vegetables than any cook in history. In tricking the concealed nutrition into my brother and me, her philosophy for every new casserole was, "How do you know you don't like it if you don't taste it? After all, even scripture says, 'Taste and see . . .'"

So seeing is believing.

Sometimes.

But then there are times that believing is seeing.

The Master Eye Doctor said to one of His patients, "Except a man be born again, he cannot see the Kingdom of God." There is a dimension and view of life that only faith can understand. Without that faith, we waste our potential. We are like three-way lamps using one-way bulbs.

Not long ago I was busy doing my own thing my own way. When I finished the day, I found my bootstraps had taken me their usual distance. "Well, I can always learn from my mistakes," I said proudly, bumping my head on the low overhang of the pantry door . . . again. (I think I have perfect vision in one eye. I just can't remember which one.) So I need faith.

I'm reminded of a little boy born blind who had a delicate operation performed on his eyes. When at last the healing from the operation had taken its course and the bandages were removed, the little boy was led into a garden where his gaze fell on
> tall swaying pines,
> > bowers of roses,
> bunches of daises,
> beds of violets,
and waterlillies that floated in pools of azure blue.

In absolute delight he exclaimed to his mother, who was standing close by, "Why didn't you tell me it was so beautiful?"

Through her tears she replied, "I tried to, my son, but you couldn't see. You were blind."

6

WILL THE REAL YOU PLEASE STAND UP - I
YEAH-BUTS and WHAT-IFS

O.K. Get out your Old Testaments. You know . . . the front of The Book where guys hide love notes and the girls press flowers.

Today we're checking at Daniel 11:32. In the last half of this short verse there are mentioned seven types of people, everybody in this room.

Here it is: "But the people who do know their God shall be strong and do exploits."

There you have it . . . seven kinds of people right there.

"But the people that do know their God shall be strong and do exploits."

Don't go any farther than the first word for the first group: "BUT . . ." That's right, the objectors. No matter where you go or who you work with, you'll always find a good supply of these folks who think nothing should be done for the first time.

You know . . . We've never done it that way before.

Or . . . if it ain't broke, don't fix it.

Or . . . wait till this hits the fan. Do you have any idea how much trouble this will be?

It may be a great idea . . . BUT . .

They remind me of Arnold. It was in 1878 that Arnold stood by the first railroad train he had ever seen. The line of cars stretched down the track and out of sight. Arnold watched with great interest and extreme doubt as the crew scurried around making last minute adjustments.

The engine was belching steam and hissing madly. He chuckled out loud as the engineer pushed forward on the throttle. Sparks were flying everywhere while the wheels spun going nowhere.

"You'll never get it started," Arnold shouted. "A contraption like that can't work." The man in the cab grinned and put the engine in reverse to take up slack, released some sand on the tracks for better traction and shoved forward again.

The big locomotive lurched up the tracks. Couplings were slamming noisily against each other as the train picked up speed. Arnold watched with unbelieving eyes. He began trotting along with the engine and soon was running all out.

He had one last warning for the engineer as the train pulled ahead: "You'll never get it stopped!!"

Did you ever meet Arnold? If you ever tried to make a dream come true, you did! He's the one who orders tuna salad . . . and expects to get Charlie. He'll forget that Babe Ruth hit 714 home runs in his career and only remember that he struck out twice that often.

A fisherman friend told me that no one needs a top for a crab basket. If one crab starts to climb up the side of the basket, the other crabs will reach up and pull it back down.

Arnold somehow seems compelled to keep everyone working on the same monument to mediocrity. But some of us won't listen to Arnold's gospel.

There is a pull upward in the Master's words:
"Ask what you will . . ."
"Choose you this day . . ."
"All things are possible to him that believes . . .."

So why not go out on a limb? Isn't that where the fruit is?

Of course there are problems with dreaming and reaching. But nothing worthwhile is ever achieved without patience, labor, and possibly, disappointments.

Stars may be seen from the bottom of a deep well, when they cannot be seen from the top of the mountain. You just have to keep your eyes open, that's all.

Besides, the men who try to do something and fail are infinitely better than those who try to do nothing and succeed.

The key to success in life is focus. Concentrate on your task.Obstacles are those frightening things that you see when you take your eyes off the goal.

Before Woody Hayes came to coach football at Ohio State in the 50's, he had been coaching at the much smaller Universities of Denison and Miami in Ohio. "The first time I stood in the middle of the OSU stadium with its 86,000 seats staring down at me," he recalls, "I was really shook up. My young son was with me holding my hand. He must have felt my reaction, because he said, "But Daddy, the football field is still the same size.'"

Take that, Arnold!

And you know, when you check back in Scripture, those "yeah-but" guys were the ones who took the children of Israel on a 40 year hike through the wilderness.

When the spies came back from looking over the Promised Land, their lips were overflowing with good news and praise for all that they had seen. A land flowing with milk and honey, abundant food and nourishment and clusters of grapes so huge it took two men to carry one bunch.

Joshua and Caleb were ecstatic . . . ready to move immediately. It was the other 10 spies who hesitated, contemplated and negated.

"All these good things are true," they affirmed. "But there are giants in the land . . . and we seem like grasshoppers in their sight."

You caught that word of discouragement, didn't you? "BUT!"

"It's true . . . BUT!"

"It's wonderful . . . BUT!"

"We know God made it for us . . . BUT!"

And the assembly heard the objectors and stayed in the wilderness . . . for 40 years. When Paul sums up their history for the Corinthians, he says that with many of them, "God was not well pleased."

And that's putting it mildly. Not pleased. Of the original cast of pilgrims who left Egypt and decided to stay in the desert . . . do you know how many made it into the Promised Land? Of the 3,000,000 who started . . . there were only two . . . Joshua and Caleb . . . who walked across the Jordan into the Land that

God had promised. All the rest of the "starters" died in the wilderness as objectors. To say "God was not pleased with them" is on the underside of a heavy indictment.

The Children of Israel who took the Land were those who were born on the trip . . . plus the two men who followed a dream. It's better to be a "Promised Land grasshopper with wings" than a "desert-bound ground hog with holes."

7

GOOD LOOKING or
LOOKING GOOD

We're still in the Old Testament continuing our look at seven categories of people everywhere (forget everywhere, we're talking right here). So back to Daniel 11:32 again.

You know . . . if reincarnation were even a remote possibility, there are three things I would not want to come back as:

> the front pew of a church,
> the third verse of a hymn,
> or one of the Old Testament prophets.

None of them are ever used! Look at Daniel 11:32 as we proceed to the second of these character types.

First there was "BUT" . . . the Objectors. Now . . . the second group . . . but "THE PEOPLE". These are the Onlookers. Just THE PEOPLE.

You know . . . atmosphere. The folks who are there, but not quite involved. Kind of like spiritual wallpaper . . . just hanging around.

They are always ready to take credit for whatever goes on, but never responsibility for whatever goes down.

Didn't "we" have a great meeting . . . .
Didn't "we" reach a lot of people . . .
Didn't "we" get a lot accomplished . . .

They remind you of a football game where 22 men in perfect condition run up and down the field while 75,000 fans who need the exercise pay to sit and watch . . . then go home exhausted and voiceless from all the cheering.

And at the office coffee-break on Monday, those are the people who are sure to let everyone know that "we" played a great game . . . and that "we" are surely in contention for a National Championship.

But you know there's no ownership without involvement.

People who observe from the sidelines . . . in sports or in service . . . are shallow at best and hollow at least.

Have you heard this quote from Mother Teresa?

"Duty is a very personal thing. It is what comes from knowing the need to take action and not just a need to urge others to do something."

Great occasions for helping others come seldom . . .
 . . . but small ones surround us daily.

This is a story about 4 people named
EVERYBODY,
SOMEBODY,
ANYBODY
and NOBODY.

There was an important job to be done and EVERY-BODY was sure that SOMEBODY would do it. ANYBODY would have done it but NOBODY did it.

SOMEBODY got angry about that, because it was EVERYBODY'S job. EVERYBODY thought ANYBODY should do it, but NOBODY realized that EVERYBODY blamed SOMEBODY when NOBODY did what ANYBODY could have done.

These gentlemen were all neighbors but the way they lived was a shame. The all went to the same church but you never could have enjoyed worshipping with any of them.

EVERYBODY stayed home on Sundays to go fishing or to visit with his friends. ANYBODY wanted to worship but was afraid that SOMEBODY wouldn't speak to him. So . . . NOBODY went to church.

Actually, NOBODY was the only decent one of the four. NOBODY did all the church visitation and NOBODY volunteered anytime there was a church building or property work project.

And one day a Sunday School teacher was needed. EVERYBODY thought ANYBODY could do it. SOMEBODY thought EVERYBODY should. Guess who did . . . NOBODY!

And then one day a fifth neighbor moved in to live among them. EVERYBODY felt SOMEBODY should win him to Christ. ANYBODY could have at least made an effort. You want to guess who finally did win him? That's right . . . NOBODY!!

It is only by getting out of the stands and into the arena of life that fulfillment and satisfaction can be realized. That's what gives you perspective for living . . . and establishes the priorities you need for balance.

It is illusion to think that more comfort means more happiness. Happiness comes from the capacity to feel deeply,
to enjoy simply,
to think freely,
and to be needed.

And until you have loved someone more than yourself . . .
. . . you have not loved.

But THE PEOPLE . . . the ordinary onlookers . . . never seem to comprehend the need for stability or commitment. THE PEOPLE can be moved by fad or craze. Those are the folks whom the Apostle James calls "doubleminded men, unstable in all their ways."

You know . . . just hard to pin down.

For instance . . . beware of polls and pollsters. The usually are done of, by and for THE PEOPLE. And sophisticated tabulators can get any answer they want with loaded questions. Take this example:

Most people vote NO when asked if they approved of smoking while praying. But the vote turned to YES when the same people were asked if they approved of praying while smoking.

You might as well ask a group of turkeys what they think they should be stuffed with next November. It sure won't be bread crumbs, celery, onions, sausage and giblets.

As experts on turkey stuffing, those birds would vote unanimously for bugs, worms and grit! HAPPY THANKS-GIVING.

So even experts don't necessarily know what's right for all of us. Because most of them are onlookers. They're THE PEOPLE, trying their best to see which way the wind is blowing, rather than trying to capture it and make it blow for us . . . not just at us.

But can we all agree on this truth? We need to get back to basics. Everybody started out pretty much the same. Some just stopped sooner.

Our next door neighbor was only 5 when he fell out of bed. His cries of frightened surprise aroused his whole household. (Didn't do much for the serenity of the rest of the community, either.)

After Mother had him safely tucked back under the covers she asked the obvious: "Why did you fall out of bed?"

Between the sobs he replied, "I guess I went to sleep too close to where I got in."

For so many of THE PEOPLE, the start is made with love, enthusiasm and excitement. But like a little boy climbing into bed, we stay too close to the edge.

The very nature of life is progress and growth. Sometimes it seems that down here on earth the journey is the goal. God has provided plateaus and oases, pleasant places for reflecting on the view of both past and future, and refreshing for the present.

Plenty of stopping places . . . but no parking places.

Oliver Cromwell had this motto carved to hang on his wall:

**IF I CEASE BEING BETTER
I CEASE BEING GOOD**

8

GOOD-DOERS or
DO-GOODERS

You remember . . . we're finding seven qualities of character by examining Daniel 11:32, "But the people that do know their God shall be strong and do exploits."

> First, the Objectors . . . "BUT"
> Then, the Onlookers . . . "But the PEOPLE"
> Now, the Workers . . . "But the people that **DO**"

There is a high priority in Scripture for partners in the vineyard. People who lend a hand,
> give a shove,
> help a friend.

> Those who know what to do,
> how to do it,
> when it should be done.

I found this the other day on a warehouse office wall:

> We the willing
> led by the unknowing
> are doing the impossible

for the ungrateful.
We have done so much
for so long
with so little,
we are now qualified
to do anything
with nothing.

There's a wonderful urgency of persistence there. People who **DO** somehow keep on doing. Another office wall hanging here. See if you can guess who said it.

PRESS ON . . . nothing in the world can take the place of persistence.

TALENT WILL NOT . . . nothing is more common than unsuccessful men with talent.

GENIUS WILL NOT . . . unrewarded genius is almost a proverb.

EDUCATION WILL NOT . . . the world is full of educated derelicts.

Persistence and determination alone are omnipotent!!!

Ray Kroc, Founder
MacDonald's

Have you ever noticed how many people don't want to try anything new because they have a low feeling of expectancy. So afraid of misfiring. . . they never even take aim . . . let alone shoot.

But here's some good news . . . if at first you don't succeed, you're running about average.

Out of the first 4 stores F. W. Woolworth opened, 3 failed. But he kept at it and when he died, he was worth over $20,000,000.

Admiral Peary attempted to reach the North Pole on seven different trips before he made it on the eighth.

Thomas Edison tried 1600 different materials before settling on carbon as the filament in the electric light bulb.

Oscar Hammerstein had 5 flop shows that lasted less than 6 weeks each before Oklahoma. And that success ran 269 weeks for 2,248 performances and grossed 7,000,000.

Willie Mays didn't get a hit in his first 26 times at bat in the Major Leagues. But on his next try he got a home run off Warren Spahn.

John Creasey, one of the world's most successful novelists, whose 560 books have sold 60,000,000 copies, collected 743 rejection slips from publishers before he managed to get one word in print.

George Bernard Shaw was a bad speller in school.
Benjamin Franklin and Picasso were poor mathematicians.
Einstein was expelled from school for being "mentally slow".
And so were Poe, Shelley and Whistler.

Eddy Arcaro lost the first 100 horse races he rode in, and everybody knows that Babe Ruth hit 714 home runs. But did you remember that he struck out almost twice that many times getting them?

You see, it's better to try to do something and fail, than to try to do nothing and succeed! There are plenty of rules for success, but none of them work unless you do.

It's not how fast you start the race that matters. It's how you finish that really counts.

What God really wants is partners.

I've had that feeling about God and me ever since I read that He said, "Hence forth I call you not servants, for the servant knoweth not what his Lord doeth; but I have called you friends." (John 15:15)

It seems that He wants to share in my life,
to help in my decisions,
to guide in my directions
but not to do it all for me.

God has left me with some responsibility. And it usually seems that what I do must happen first.

I resist the devil	God causes him to flee from me.
I practice my songs	God uses them to bless people.
I study for my exams	God calls facts to my memory.
I begin walking	God directs my path.

Cooperation is a valid spiritual concept. I do something and God does something and the real successes come as we work on the same things at the same times from different ends. God expects me to do all I can . . .
then He does the rest.
I work like everything depends on me . . .
and I pray like everything depends on Him.

When we share together . . . God and I . . . good things happen. And that's why Jesus calls us friends.

A farmer was homesteading some wilderness property. There were rocks and gullies and thorns and weeds everywhere. He scraped and cleaned and leveled and plowed and planted and watered for nearly a year. His pastor came out and looked at the fine crop and said, "God surely has blessed you with a beautiful farm on this land." "You could say that," the farmer replied, "but the place sure didn't look this good when God had it by Himself!!"

So you just have to keep working . . . and moving. If you sit still, eventually you'll be run over even if you are on the right track.

> If I should stumble . . . as I have and will,
>   Oh, let me stumble going up the hill;
> Let the stumbling be because my eyes
>   Are fixed upon some star high in the skies.
>
> If I should fall . . . and I will have my share,
>   Let me fall going up the stair;
> And let me not blame others for the pain,
>   But quietly arise and try again.
>
> If I should trip . . . let it be, I seek,
>   A precious foothold toward a mountain peak;
> Help me remember that if I stumble and fall not quite,
>   I gain a step toward the mountain height.

9

USE IT or LOSE IT

So here we are at character description number 4 in our exploration of Daniel 11:32. "But the people that do know their God shall be strong and do exploits."

1. "BUT" . . . the Objectors.
2. "But the PEOPLE" . . . the Onlookers.
3. "But the people that DO" . . . the Workers.
4. Now for the "people that do KNOW" . . . the Thinkers.

"You don't have to check in your brains when you believe in Jesus." One of my good friends, Don Howarth, said that to me. Then he was a brilliant student in the Harvard Law School, now he's the President of his own law firm in Los Angeles.

We were discussing the seeming dilemma that so many college students face trying to balance academia with biblical truth. Don's approach was (and is) to start with truth and expand it, not experiment with information and then try to cram it into verity.

"God is not afraid of my question . . . nor intimidated by my quest. After all, He's the One who said, 'Come, let us

reason together, though your sins be as scarlet, they shall be as white as wool.'"

Don went on, "He invited me to think it through with Him when He asked Paul to write, 'I beseech you therefore, brethren, by the mercies of God, that ye present your bodies a living sacrifice, holy, acceptable unto God, which is your reasonable service.'"

"Using my brains to strengthen my faith was His idea . . . not mine."

Thank you, Don.

Thank you, God.

And to get you more current, just the other day I was talking to someone who was having a difficult time offering a logical explanation for a questionable attitude. Finally, in a desperate attempt to justify his position, he pointed to the region of his belt buckle and firmly asserted, "I feel it in here." And I felt sorry for the man whose logic was left to the mercy of his stomach.

But he's not alone . . . millions of people are doing the same thing today. No wonder so many are learning to spell Rolaids. They're improving their thinking.

Instead of reaching into their minds to prove a point they're pointing to their innards. The head which was intended to be the commander-in-chief of thinking has now surrendered to navel operations.

But God never intended that! Let me say it again, you don't have to check in your brains when you believe in Jesus. To tell the truth, you'd better not! Because faith is always built on fact . . . and it is reason that helps us sort out those facts.

Faith is not belief without proof; it is trust without reservation. And that trust comes from the knowledge of His past record.

One summer when Julie was still less than 2 years old, I was leading the music at Redwood Christian Camp in the beautiful Santa Cruz mountains in California. We were playing together one afternoon outside the tabernacle while a Ladies' Missionary Rally was being conducted inside.

A lady on the program panel was a little late and came hurrying around the building planning to use a rickety back staircase with no railing and rotting steps. She was absolutely horrified to see Julie standing at the top . . . teetering back and forth . . . with no Daddy in sight.

Not wanting to startle the youngster by crying out, she quietly ran toward the staircase . . .but to no avail. Julie leaned a little too far forward and fell off the edge of the little landing at the top of the stairs.

The concerned lady never broke stride as she rounded the steps and came around the back of the platform expecting to find a crushed, bleeding little girl.

Instead . . . she found Julie in my arms. That sweet little less-than-two-year-old had jumped off the porch into my eager grasp.

With adrenaline squirting out of her ears, the lady sputtered, "Little girl, why did you jump like that?"

And with all the confidence of a protected child, safe in her Father's arms, Julie looked the lady right in the eye and said, "My Daddy told me to."

You see, Julie was a jumper. She'd jump from anything into my arms. Out of her crib, from the fender of a parked car, off the edge of a swimming pool. It didn't matter where . . . she just loved to leap.

So that day at the camp when I asked her to jump from the stairs eight feet down into my arms . . . she never hesitated. To the lady it was frightening . . . but to Julie it was a way of life. It never occurred to her that I might not catch her. Me, either. I never had dropped her before, so why should she have second thoughts now?

See . . . that's trust without reservation. Based on past history, I said "Jump" . . . and she did.

Not because she didn't have any brains. But because she didn't have any fear. She didn't know anything better to do than to trust her Daddy.

Faith is always a thoughtful decision based on past experience. It's not a fanciful leap off a towering diving board into the darkness, while at the same time hoping there's water in the pool. Where God has proven Himself faithful before, He will again. Count on it.

God gave you that grey matter in your head to do more than hold your ears apart. When He said, "Lean not to your own understanding" He did not mean, "use not your own understanding."

Think about it.

10

KNOW GOD or NO GOD

And here comes number five. If you just jumped in with us, we are studying the Old Testament verse written over 2500 years ago by Prophet Daniel . . . to be opened at a later date. This is the time. Daniel 11:32, "But the people that do know their God, shall be strong and do exploits."

> The Objectors . . . . "BUT"
> The Onlookers . . . . "but the PEOPLE"
> The Workers   . . . . "but the people that DO"
> The Thinkers . . . . "but the people that do KNOW"
> And now, #5   . . . . "but the people that do know
>   THEIR GOD".

They are the Possessors.

We're talking serious fundamentals here. You can't go any place until you pass through this door. The absolute epitome of all truth. You must know Him . . . in a personal way.

Otherwise, you'll be like Sheldon.

> He brushed his teeth twice a day . . . with a
> nationally advertised tooth paste.
> The doctors examined him twice a year.
> He kept his feet dry when it rained.
> He slept with the windows open.
> He stuck to a diet with plenty of fresh vegetables
> and high in fiber.
> He relinquished his tonsils and traded in several
> worn-out organs.
> He golfed . . . but never more than 18 holes at a time.
> He got at least eight hours sleep every night.
> He never smoked, drank nor lost his temper.
> He did his "daily dozen" daily.
> He was all set to live to be more than a hundred.
> The other day he stepped on a banana peel and landed
> on his head.

> The funeral will be held Wednesday.

> He is survived by eighteen specialists,
> four health clubs,
> six gymnasiums and
> numerous manufacturers
> of health foods
> and antibiotics.

He forgot God,
> lived as if this world was all there was,
> and neglected his eternal welfare.

> He is now with those who say, "The harvest is past,
> the summer is ended,
> and we are not saved."
> Jeremiah 8:20

We all have a tendency to assume that we can do anything. (And if necessity is the mother of invention, then assumption is the father of all screw ups.) Confidence in our own abilities has taught us to stretch

and reach

and plan

and dream.

Anything is possible . . . if we just make it happen!

"Please, I'd rather do it myself," was intended to be an advertising slogan a few years ago. But have you noticed how many people have adopted it as a life-philosophy? It's kinda scary.

When Jeri was 4, I felt that sometimes her tongue ran a little out of control. In a fatherly effort to keep her mouth from being labeled "OPENED BY MISTAKE", I decided that suppertime was as good an opportunity as any other to enforce thoughtful restraint. When she let out a few ill-chosen sassy words, I dismissed her from the table to her bedroom with the advice, "Don't come back 'til you can be a good girl."

In less than a minute she had returned to her chair, laughing, giggling, and in a few seconds, sassing. Again to her bedroom, admonished sternly, "Don't come back 'til you can be good!"

Ninety-three seconds later (I timed her) she was back nibbling at the food and testing me. When the sassy words came again, I helped her down from the chair and gave her a little physical assistance down the hall (we believed in the scriptural ordinance of the laying on of hands in our house) and told her again, "Don't come back until you can be A GOOD GIRL!!"

We finished dinner alone and I felt I needed to check things out in the bedroom. I never intended for her to stay there; I only wanted her to be good.

I found her leaning against her bed . . . sobbing. I asked why she hadn't come back and she looked at me through her tears, touched my cheek with a chubby finger and said, "Daddy, by myself I just don't know how to be good."

And that's well said for all of us. Try as we will to "be good", we all need help . . . from outside of ourselves . . . from above.

That's because God without man is still God; but man without God is nothing at all.

I was one of the crowd. Just a spectator that one warm evening on the UCLA campus. The 700 of us had gathered to hear Madeline Murray O'Hare, champion of atheistic causes explain her position.

I knew I couldn't accept what she said or defend her philosophy, but I wanted to be there. I knew there were lessons of communication I needed to learn and I was anxious to know how she would deal with these people.

Even before she walked out on the stage I felt my attitude turn antagonistic. I felt out of place and conspicuous . . . like a ham and cheese sandwich in a Jewish deli. But just then she appeared and I knew I had to wait it out.

After the meeting I measured my attitude again. I had really enjoyed the evening, and, surprisingly, Miss O'Hare had shed some light on a number of definitions for me.

The most important thing she said was, "I am an atheist, not because I have searched behind every star and looked under every rock to prove there is no God. I am an atheist because I live my life as if there were no God."

And I thought to myself . . . how many Church members and professing Christians do I know who live exactly that way . . . AS IF there were no God. Believers . . . never stopping to ask, or stooping to serve or pausing to think.

Better your life should be like the man born blind, described in John, chapter 9. Jesus made some mud, daubed it on those sightless eyes and sent him to wash in the pool of Siloam.

When the man returned with perfect vision, the sceptics grilled him for information.

Why was this done to you on the Sabbath?
  Is He who healed you a Prophet?
    Where is He from?
      What is His name?

Hear and heed the answer. Eternity depends on it.

"I don't know His name or His background.
  I don't know His hometown.
  I don't even know why He did this.

  But one thing I do know . . .
  Once I was blind . . .
  Now I see . . .

    I know that ! ! !

11

WILL THE REAL YOU PLEASE STAND UP (VI)
STAND FOR SOMETHING
or FALL FOR ANYTHING

And here's #6 in our list of personality-types from Daniel 11:32.

So far:

#1. "BUT!"........ .... OBJECTORS
#2. "but THE PEOPLE!" .... ONLOOKERS
#3. "but the people that DO!" .... WORKERS
#4. "but the people that do KNOW!"........ THINKERS
#5. "but the people that do know THEIR GOD!" ...
                                              POSSESSORS
And now #6
"but the people that do know their God, shall be STRONG!"

They are the WITHSTANDERS!

We're not talking physical prowess here. This is inner strength.
              The ability to see life through . . .
       to acknowledge there is a higher power than yours
        to accept that bad things happen to good people

and that God has a plan and a promise to work
everything out for our good and His Glory.

That's called strength. It's based on commitment, proven
in faithfulness, and honored in serenity.

Commitment at any level of life needs to be definite,
constant and reaffirmed. Pity the wife who wondered why her
husband never said he loved her.
"I told you that 30 years ago when we got married," he
grumbled. "If anything changes . . . I'll let you know."
Commitment is like eggs . . . smells bad if not kept fresh.

Maybe you remember the young suitor, on his knees
before the girl he loved, promising,
"I'd swim the widest river for you.
I'd cross the hottest desert for you.
I'd scale the tallest mountain for you.
I love you so much,
I'd risk anything to win your favor and your hand."

"Oh," she sighed. "Would you give your life for me?"
"No," he confessed. "Mine is an undying love."

You know . . . love is not a rock.
Love is like bread . . . made fresh every day.

I was in the waiting room of the dentist office . . . reading.
I came upon a story in an old magazine (did you ever find a
new one in any waiting room?) that caught my eye . . . and my
heart.

A Coast Guard crew was called on a dark, boisterous night to search for the survivors of a sinking ship. One crew member looked at the waves and supposed out loud, "We'll never get back." The Captain overheard the remark and brushed it aside by saying, "We don't have to come back.

We only have to go."

That's what you call FAITHFULNESS. It is the basic quality of worth-whileness.

Sticking to a commitment . . .

Seeing it through to the finish . .

Even when you think no one's watching.

It is day by day living . . . sometimes through criticism
                                          and ridicule,
                                   and weariness
                                   and loneliness,
                            and heartbreak
                            and misunderstanding.

But no matter what. . . . tenaciously,
                                   ruggedly,
                                   stubbornly
                                   holding on.

The world is crowded with little people who do nothing without recognition, who fear mistakes, and who refuse to do more than they're paid to do. They're the people who start clearing the desk of life at five till five. They stay little and won't be missed when they're gone.

I guess that's why Paul said, "Take the things you've learned and commit them to faithful men who will teach others."

Here's a classy example of faithfulness . . . a simple definition of dedication. Guess what it is without peeking.

I represent my country.
 I'm always ready for service.
  I go wherever I'm sent.
   I do what I'm asked to do.
    I stick to my task until it's done.
     I don't strike back when I'm struck.
      I don't give up when I'm licked.
       I'm necessary to the happiness of the world.
        I keep up to date.
         I find no job too small.
          I work well on a team for big jobs.
           I'm crowned with a mark of service.

I am a Postage Stamp!

Not bad for a little guy. How 'bout us bigger ones. Here's one for us all . . .

When the 1900's were still in their teens, Luther B. Bridgers was a popular song-writer, singing-evangelist travelling the revival/campmeeting circuit. One of his songs was being sung in churches and religious meetings from coast to coast. In its original form, it had four verses and a chorus:

There's within my heart a melody,
Jesus whispers sweet and low,
"Fear not, I am with thee, peace be still,"
In all of life's ebb and flow.
All my life was wrecked by sin and strife,
Discord filled my heart with pain;

Jesus swept across the broken strings,
Stirred the slumbering chords again.

Feasting on the riches of His grace,
Resting 'neath His shelt'ring wing;
Always looking on His smiling face,
That is why I shout and sing.

Soon He's coming back to welcome me,
Far beyond the starry sky,
I shall wing my flight to worlds unknown,
I shall reign with Him on High.

Chorus
Jesus, Jesus, Jesus,
Sweetest name I know;
Fills my every longing,
Keeps me singing as I go.

The fifth verse was written six years after the song was first published and made popular. But it is that final verse (now listed as verse four in most hymnals) that shows the real meaning of the song that Jesus gives and the depth of character that plumbed the soul of L. B. Bridgers.

Returning to his home in Kansas after a week long meeting, he noticed from the train window that a fire was burning fiercely in his city. He paused a moment to offer prayer for the people involved in that tragedy.

Stepping into a carriage that would take him to his house, he noticed the fire was in his section of town. Getting closer, the fire was noticeably on his street, and as he turned the last corner, he realized it was his house wildly ablaze.

Leaping from the carriage, he was restrained by the

neighbors. One of them said, "It's over. There's nothing you can do. You've lost everything."

"What do mean . . . everything?" he asked.

Softly and slowly the neighbor answered, "Everything . . . your house, your possessions, your wife and your two children. Everything."

L. B. Bridgers sat alone on a stump in his front yard in stunned silence, the smoke still rising from the embers of what had been his home . . . his life. Then, without getting up, he took some paper from his pocket, and wrote these words for his favorite song:

Though sometimes He leads through waters deep,
Trials fall across the way;
Though sometimes the path seems rough and steep,
See His footprints all the way.

Now that's what we call . . . strong.

12

ACQUIRING EXCUSES or ACHIEVING EXPLOITS

And you thought we'd never make it. I mean all the way to #7. But here we are . . . and doesn't it feel good.

Check it over again with me . . . one more time. Daniel 11:32: "But the people that do know their God shall be strong and do exploits."

OBJECTORS.."BUT!"
ONLOOKERS...................................."but THE PEOPLE!"
WORKERS.................................."but the people that DO!"
THINKERS......................"but the people that do KNOW!"
POSSESSORS....."but the people that do know THEIR GOD!"
WITHSTANDERS".."but the people that do know their God shall be STRONG!"

And now, the seventh and last type of person described in that verse. "But the people that do know their God shall be strong and **DO EXPLOITS.**"

These are THE CONQUERORS!

While most people make excuses . . . conquerors achieve
exploits. No matter what the situation, they have learned to
come out on top. Not because of any greatness of theirs . . .
but by a greatness in them.

These are the fellowship Paul describes as
"zealous of good works"
constrained by the love of Christ"
"always caused to triumph"

and whom the critics described in the Book of Acts as
"those who turned the world upside down."

Believers were intended to be part of an infinite
powerful
exciting
living body
known as the called out ones
. . . God's ecclesia.

Before the foundations of the world were laid,
before the morning stars broke forth in chorus,
before the foot of man ever walked on the sands of time,
the Church was a warm place in the heart of God.

The company of the redeemed,
the fellowship of the saints,
the gathering of the bloodwashed pilgrims
has always been special to the Father.

His children, through faith, subdued kingdoms,
brought righteousness,
obtained promises,
stopped the mouths of lions,
quenched the violence of fire,
escaped the edge of the sword;
out of weakness were made strong,
waxed valiant in fight,
turned to flight the armies of aliens.

They were stoned,
sawn asunder,
tempted,
bribed,
and slain by the sword.

The Church has outlasted
outbelieved
outlived her earthly critics and enemies.

Men have sought to destroy her message,
nullify her hope,
injure her mission,
bury her mercy,
kill her love.

But if God be for Her. . . Who can be against Her?
She is the candlestick,
the assembly of saints,
the bride,
the called,
the elect,
the faithful.

She is justified,
    ransomed,
      redeemed,
        precious,
          pure,
            sanctified.

The Church is known as the flock of God,
    the friends of God,
    the glory of God,
    the image of God,
    the treasure of God.

She is the joy of the whole earth,
    lively stones in the habitation of God,
    members of Christ,
    light of the world,
    salt of the earth.

The Church has been called beloved of God,
    body of Christ,
    brothers and sisters,
    sons of God,
      daughters of the King,
      joint heirs with Jesus,
      children of the
      Kingdom,
        family of God.

God calls her peaceable, yet mighty.

She is a pillar of truth,
        vessel of mercy,
             building of God.

The Church is a fellowship . . . these close at hand
                and all believers
                     everywhere
          even those who have gone on before . . .

Seeing we are surrounded with so great a cloud of witnesses.

WE ALL ARE HIS CHURCH!!!

And Jesus said: "I will build My Church,
    And the gates of Hell shall not prevail against it."

Other translations make that read:

The power of death shall not subdue it.

The forces of death shall not overpower it.

The doors of hell shall not shut in on it.

The power of Satan's world shall never overthrow it.

The gates of Hell shall not hold out against it.

The might of Hades shall not triumph over it.

"But the people
          that do know their God
                   shall be strong
                         and do exploits"

13

MINISTRY AND
MINISTERS

During a recent ecumenical gathering, someone rushed in shouting, "The building is on fire!"

. . . The Methodists gathered in a corner and prayed.

. . . The Baptists yelled, "Where is the water?"

. . . The Quakers quietly praised God for the blessing that fire brings.

. . . The Lutherans posted a notice on the door declaring the fire was evil.

. . . The Catholics took pledges to cover the damage.

. . . The Pentecostals praised God and shouted, "Holy smoke!"

. . . The Fundamentalists proclaimed, "It's the vengeance of God."

. . . The Christian Scientists agreed among themselves
that there really was no fire at all.

. . . The Presbyterians appointed a chair-person who was
to appoint a committee to look into the matter
and make a written report to the Session.

. . . The Salvation Army took their drums and brass,
formed a parade and marched out of the building.

We may all have different approaches to the same event...
but that's OK. We don't have to agree on HOW we serve
. . . just WHO we serve.

We are an uncommon people
with an uncommon faith in an uncommon God
serving in an uncommon way
while moving toward an uncommon destiny.

You remember this story? Three congregations meeting
in separate buildings at the intersection of Main and Church
Streets. The Presbyterians on one corner, the Methodists on
another and the Baptists on the third.

It was Sunday evening and the services were running
simultaneously. You could have heard the congregations
singing from four blocks down the street.

The Methodists: WILL THERE BE ANY STARS IN
                    MY CROWN?
The Baptists: NO NOT ONE
The Presbyterians: O THAT WILL BE GLORY FOR ME

We of the Church are so often like horses and donkeys. When horses are attacked, they gather in a tight circle, face each other and kick the enemy. But donkeys face the enemy . . . and kick each other.

Look at it this way. Who needs a physical fitness program? Most of us get enough exercise . . .

> jumping to conclusions
> flying off the handle
> dodging responsibilities
> bending rules
>> running down everything
>> circulating rumors
>> passing the buck
>> stirring up trouble
>>> sawing logs
>>> shooting the bull
>>> polishing the apple
>>> digging up excuses
>>>> slinging mud
>>>> throwing our weight around
>>>> beating the system
>>>> and pushing our luck.

But we all ought to find agreement on one thing . . . we do need to be ministers. As far as Jesus is concerned, we are called on as believers to CARE, and to SHARE and to DARE.

A few years ago in a gathering of United Methodist Evangelists, a famous Jewish Rabbi from New York was scheduled to speak. There was no small brouhaha . . . after all, what could a man of that faith have to say to these leaders of the Christian persuasion?

When you distill his address to its basic theme . . . the Rabbi had plenty to offer. Listen!

The world does not care one iota about the coloringof the carpet in your Sanctuary. Nor are they concerned with how many ranks you have on your pipe organ. And they do not ask the price of your stained glass windows.

The world only asks one question:

"Can you help me where I hurt?"

That is not to say, "No colorful carpets . . .
or ostentatious organs . . .
or wonderful windows . . . "

Just understand who those things are for. They all lend themselves to your contentment in Church. They create an atmosphere of pleasantness, where you can come to worship and even bring your friends comfortably into God's House. Nothing wrong with any of that. But none of those things even come close to answering what the world outside really wants to know:

"Can you help me where I hurt?"

Somehow we have arrived at a misconstrued conception that ministry success is gauged by how high up the ladder of esteem we manage to climb.

We rate ourselves by how many people know us . . .
how much influence we can wield . . .
how popular our services are . . .
who admires what we do.

Jesus never operated like that. Instead . . . His was an inverted pyramid. It was never a struggle to see who gets to the top . . . but who can reach the bottom? Who can be the greatest servant? Who can show the most love? Unconditional love, at that.

Remember in John 13 when Jesus approached the disciples in the room of the Last Supper. He was wearing a towel around His waist and carried a basin of water.

Peter asked, "What's going on here?"
Jesus answered, "It's time to wash feet."
Peter smirked, "I'm not washing feet. Not even yours."
Jesus responded, "I know. I'm washing yours."

Ministry is never getting to the top. It is always serving at the bottom.

In Re'Gen, we used to have a cross-stitched expression hanging on the inside door of the wardrobe section of our truck, so everybody had to face it everyday. It was an obvious truth posted in an inescapable place.

IT'S NICE TO BE IMPORTANT . . .
BUT IT'S MORE IMPORTANT TO BE NICE!

And here's another ministry truth for you:
Thoughtfulness of others is the basis of ministry.
Helpfulness to others is the expression of ministry.

Dr. Orval Butcher, the founding Pastor of Skyline Wesleyan Church in San Diego was my ministry teacher, mentor and influence. And he is still the "main man" in my spiritual life and growth. He could find more lessons about compassion and concern than anyone since Jesus Himself.

Like this one . . . at staff coffee one Monday morning, when he suspended our casual conversation with this gentle insistence.

"Yesterday morning after the 11 o'clock Service, while we were greeting our people, I felt a tug at my coat. I turned around to see who was there. No one. I thought I had been mistaken, so I resumed the greetings.

Then . . . the tug again. This time I turned and looked down. Little Amy." (The staff favorite. Four years old, bright eyed, and a smile that lit up the whole world.)

"I knelt down beside her," Pastor Butcher continued. "She didn't say a word . . . just held out her little finger to me. It was vividly wrapped in a Mickey Mouse Bandaid. I peeled the bandage off and there was a little cut on the tip of her pinky. I held it close, kissed it gently, and wrapped the bandaid around it again. We smiled at each other and she ran to find her Mommy.

"Now boys," he said speaking to his staff, "everything you need to know about Ministry and Pastoral Theology is right there.

Number 1: She wasn't afraid of me.

Number 2: She knew I would care.

Number 3: She knew I would do something about it."

And I thought to myself, "I could have made two out of three on that test. I'm smart enough to kneel down next to Amy. And I'm sensitive enough to pull the bandage off. But to kiss the cut . . . to help her where she hurt . . . I'm not sure I ever would have thought of that on my own."

But I always did after that!

Evangeline Booth, daughter of the Founder of the Salvation Army, was scrubbing the sores of a drunken woman in a squalid slum when a friend said, "I wouldn't do that for a million dollars."

Evangeline replied, "I wouldn't either."

14

THE WAY OUT WEIGH IN

It's not just here in the USA that the local morticians live off the fat of the land. It is a dilemma that girdles the globe.

But right here in the Land of the Greed and the Home of the Crave, it is estimated by the boys with the slide rules that over 80 million Americans are over-weight (these are round figures of course) and that 30 million of them are in real physical danger.

The toughest part of dieting isn't watching what you eat. It's watching what your friends eat!

Of course, we all know that the culprit in this battle of the bulge is the calorie. And a calorie is nothing more than the amount of heat it takes to raise the temperature of one gram of water one degree centigrade. When you get too many calories in your system, you store them for future use and, like the person who swallowed the thermometer, you start dying by degrees.

If you're a normal American, crushed by epicurean temptation and overwhelmed with gastronomic guilt, you'll understand this plea.

SUPPERTIME SUPPLICATION

Lord, my soul is ripped with riot
Incited by my wicked diet.
"We are what we eat!" said a wise old man;
And Lord, if that's true, I'm a garbage can.

    I want to rise on judgment day, that's plain;
    But at my present weight, I'll need a crane.
    So grant me strength that I may not fall
    Into the clutches of cholesterol.

        May my flesh with carrot-sticks be sated,
        So that my soul may be polyunsaturated.
        Please show me the light that I may bear witness
        To the President's Council on Physical Fitness,

            So that at oleomargarine I'll never mutter,
            Because the road to hell is paved with butter.
            And cream is cursed, and cake is awful,
            And Satan is lurking in every waffle.

                Mephistopheles hides in provolone;
                And the devil resides in each slice of baloney.
                Beelzebub is a chocolate drop
                And Lucifer is a lollipop.

                    Give me this day my daily slice
                    But cut it thin and toast it twice.
                    I beg upon my dimpled knees:
                    Deliver me from jujubes.

And when my days of trial are done
And my war with malted milks is won,
Let me stand with your heavenly throng
In a shining robe . . . size 42 long.

    I can do it, Lord, if you'll show to me
    The virtues of lettuce and celery;
    If you'll teach me the evil of mayonnaise
    And the sinfulness of hollandaise.

        Of Pasta ala milannaise,
        Potatoes ala Lyonnaise
        And crisp-fried chicken from the south.
        Lord, if you love me, shut my mouth.

But, while you're still confined to living on this overstuffed Planet Earth, joining a local chapter of Avoirdupois Anonymous is a possibility. You remember them . . . and their slogan:

"Eat, drink and be merry, for tomorrow we diet!"

With your membership card you get a free calorie counter and the privilege of competing for the annual No-Belly Prize. Weight experts have divided mankind into three physical types:

        ECTOMORPHS . . . .the thin people
        ENDOMORPHS . . . . the fat people
        MESOMORPHS . . . the burly people

(The Greek word MORPH, meaning FORM, is the basis for these terms, plus three Greek prefixes . . . ECTO, ENDO and MESO.

ECTO means EXTERIOR, suggesting that the thin person has his weight outside. It never got inside, therefore he is thin.

MESO means MIDDLE, implying that the mesomorph carries his weight at the halfway point.

You can guess where the endomorph has his.

But you should never say diet! At least in one weighty territory of your life. That's right . . . the Bible declares it's a blessing to be fat! That's the really "good news" to some folks.

That's right . . . fat's where it's at!

But you have to realize the Good Book is talking about something other than mammoth meals and mouth-watering morsels that add magnitude to mass.

Actually, it's referring to the condition of your soul, your spiritual life, that "hidden man of the heart."

Check this menu, straight from the book of Proverbs,

"HOW TO BEEF UP YOUR SOUL IN FOUR EASY LESSONS"

1. SELFLESSNESS "The liberal soul shall be made fat" **(11:25).**

Just another way of saying, "Give, and it shall be given unto you." That's the exact opposite of daily life where the more you take in, the bigger you get. Ministry always focuses on the concept of "outgo produces income." The point of life is never,

"What's in it for me?"
but rather,
"What's in me for it?"

2. STEADINESS **"The diligent soul shall be made fat"**
(13:14).

Take your responsibilities seriously. Are you an accountable person? Then act that way! It is time that each person assumes answerability for his/her own attitudes, actions and destiny. Have you ever found it strange that before we're part of the Church, we always blame God for everything that goes wrong? And after we are part of the Spiritual Family, then all the storms and trials that come are from Satan. "It's never my fault. There's some sort of conspiracy going on here! Somebody's out to get me." The truth is . . . take care of yourself. Neglect your body, and you'll disappear in no time. Neglect your soul, and the same tragedy takes place.

3. SWEETNESS **"A good report makes the bones fat"**
(15:30).

Here we are at personal focus again. The invisible man can't live and grow on gossip, lies and fluffy truth. Never be the "on-purpose-searcher-outer" of bad news and stormy rumors. Go the other way . . .Be the other voice. After all, happiness is like honey . . . . . you can't spread even a little bit without getting some of it on yourself. Keep your center on the Word of God, spiritual conversation, wholesome thoughts, and "whatsoever things are of good report" (Phil. 4:8).

4. SURENESS **"He who trusts God shall be made fat"**
(28:25).

Mixing faith with the Word of God always causes growth, but simply reading it without living it will never add weight to your soul. Faith is not belief without proof . . . it is trust without reservation. Faith is to be acted upon. It is always substantial. . . you know, factual and actual. "Faith is the substance of things hoped for, the evidence of things not seen." Build your whole life . . . the way you live and how you act on your trust in God.

> Faith isn't just believing
> **. . . it's also behaving.**

So . . . snack on that for a while.

Remember the story in the book of Daniel about the banquet in the Great Hall of King Belshazzar. The finger of God (which appeared only three times in all of Scripture) wrote across the Hall wall:

MENE, MENE, TEKEL, UPHARSIN.

In my fourth grade Sunday School Class, those words were immediately translated:

MEANY, MEANY, TICKLE THE PARSON.

But we had a good teacher who wouldn't let us get by with that, and we discovered the real meaning of that verse in Daniel 5:27 is "Thou art weighed in the balances . . . and art found wanting."

Hey, King Belshazzar . . . you just don't weigh enough for God! Come to think of it, we're all going to have a confrontation like that. Get ready.

Never say diet when it comes to your spiritual life!

Fill up lavishly on milk, meat and honey for the inner man. Some day you're going to need all you can get.

15

WHEN GOD DOES
THE REST

As a senior in college, I ran into Dr. Reinhardt. Somehow I had managed to avoid any of his classes during my first three years. He was recently retired from active ministry and was filling out his spiritual commitment by teaching in the classroom. His were, reputedly, the most boring classes on campus, and the only reason I enrolled was my curriculum requirement for graduation.

I cut all the classes permissible during the semester and did as little work as possible. I was determined never to let my studies interfere with my college education. Survival was the key to success in all his classes (this one being no exception).

Anyway, that year there were just two reports (I dutifully completed both) and only one exam . . . the dreaded FINAL. He was never much on giving tests . . . didn't want to spend the time on grading, I suspect.

Ill prepared, I got to the exam room with my prayer-promises all lined up. You know . . .

"Ye have not because ye ask not."
"Whatsoever ye shall ask in prayer, believing, ye shall receive."

"The effectual, fervent prayer of a righteous man
    availeth much."
"If any of you lack wisdom,, let him ask of God who
giveth to all men liberally."

Surely all of those verses ought to add up to an "A". How
about a "B"? Whatever.

One thing is certain about a Christian College . . . you
spend a lot of time in corporate prayer. In every class session
someone was called on to focus spiritual thought before the
instruction began. Two or three people would pray prior to a
test situation. And before a final . . . it was like the Day of
Pentecost revisited. Everybody wanted to share in the action.
I took a chair for Dr. Reinhardt's test in the second row and
sat up tall so he couldn't miss me. That way I was sure to be
called on for pre-final prayer.

One problem. E-v-e-r-y-b-o-d-y was sitting up straight
that day . . . just waiting to be called. I figured, "Who cares.
I can still pray in secret and use my prayer-promise-list. Might
be better that way, anyway."

But the good Doctor fooled us all. Didn't call on anyone.
Said he would pray himself.

That caused a stir in the class . . . and bedlam in my heart.
I wasn't sure he was on my side.

But little did I know how deep was my trouble until I heard
his voice. He said (in his always pompous sound), "Dear
GawDuh." (I've always had trouble trusting any person who
has to change the tone of his voice to address God.) "Dear
GawDuh, bless us all according to our preparation! Amen."

Well, that blew it for me. **According to our preparation?**
Who ever heard of a thing like that? Anybody knows that God
is supposed to help those in need. The deprived man who is
always at a loss, the uncomposed person who can't arrange his

life, the student who never has time to get ready.

I quietly wadded up my prayer-promises and dropped them on the floor. My struggle through the exam didn't take long. Without help from the Father, I wasn't up to much pencil-pushing. The test paper was turned in early and I started back to my dorm room, muttering all the way about the unfair advantage Dr. Reinhardt had taken.

Half way across the tennis court, God spoke to me. I mean it. If I ever heard the voice of God . . . this was it. I stopped dead in my tracks. You know what He said? Listen . . . "The Doctor is right. I always will bless you according to your preparation. If you are going to speak, write, sing or lead, do the best that you can do to get ready . . . and I will do the rest."

Well . . . now I was mad at God. How could He change the rules like that. No one had ever bothered to tell me about personal responsibility in preparation. Boy, did I feel ganged up on.

I guess in my head I knew He was right . . . but my heart was having a hard time with what to me was a fresh concept. But as soon as I could collect my heart and my feelings, I got some new perspective.

My thoughts were turned to that wonderful old story about Amram and Jochebed. You remember them. No? Well, how about their son . . . Moses. (I knew you'd get it with that clue.)

Exodus, Chapter 2 has the lesson. The Israelites had been in bondage for 400 years and the Egyptians were showing concern about the growth of the captive colony. In order to keep the population in check, it had been determined that no male children would be allowed to live. (That's what you call birth control with a vengeance.)

But something wonderful happened in the hearts of Amram and Jochebed when Moses entered their lives. They were convinced that this boy was to be the long-expected deliverer.

So they hid him . . . not because they were afraid . . . but because they believed. It's important you know that. Hebrews 11:23 is specific, "By FAITH Moses, when he was born, was hid three months by his parents, because they saw he was a proper child; and they were NOT AFRAID of the King's commandment."

But when that first three months were up, Moses was starting to get noisy. (Babies add light to any household . . . usually between 2 and 4 in the morning.) Something had to be changed. If the authorities found a boy-baby in the home, it would mean death to the whole family.

So what could Jochebed do? She could have crept to the shore of the Nile under the cover of night and piously prayed, "Oh God, if you want a leader for your people, here he is. You take care of him now." And then pitched him in the water. I know a lot of people who would say, "Atta girl! Great faith!!"

But that's not faith . . . that's presumption. God is not in the business of floating babies. Moses would have hit the water and drowned . . . or been eaten by a crocodile . . . or both. That's how the soldiers were killing the boy babies anyway... just tossing them into the Nile.

Never, never presume that God will do anything that we can, should and must do for ourselves.

After hiding baby Moses for those three months, Jochebed knew there was still more that she could do before God would assume the responsibility for her child's safety.

First she made an ark out of bulrushes . . . put the baby inside, pushed it into the river and said, "O.K. God . . . he's all yours."

No she didn't. That ark, crafted of loosely woven reeds

would sink under the water in moments. So she daubed it with mud and pitch to make it waterproof . . . then pushed it out into the river and said, "O.K. God . . . he's all yours."

No . . . not yet. To put a baby who had never been outside a house before, into an uncovered float would add a new dimension to the word disaster. Expose a youngster with such tender skin to the daylight sun . . . you'd have a crispy critter in 30 minutes. Mother took a blanket, covered Moses and prayed, "O.K. God, I've done all I can do. The rest is up to you . . . he's all yours now."

And then she pushed the ark into the river.

You got that? After she had done all she could do . . . then she could expect God to move on her behalf.

And He did!

The ark drifted down the Nile and got tangled up in some bulrushes close to the shore. Now . . . here is God's Move #1. Pharaoh's daughter comes down that very morning to take a dip in the Nile River. Why in the world would this Princess choose the defiled, contaminated Nile for a bath? She had twelve bathhouses in the Palace. Count them . . . twelve! But the little girl in her spirit rose to the surface, and there she was in the weeds.

The Princess spotted the ark . . . and here is Move #2. She commanded, "Bring it to me." The servants fetched the float and she uncovered the baby. This was obviously a Jewish boy baby, and since he was a threat to her Father's Kingdom, she should have ordered the servants to simply flip the ark over, and that would have ended the story.

But do you remember what happened? The Scripture

records, "And the baby began to cry." Diaper rash? Prickly heat? Loose safety pins? We don't know why he did . . . just that he did.

And those little baby arms and legs got all tangled up in the heart strings of Pharoah's daughter. She had compassion on him . . . and picked him up. But what could she do for this little Jewish boy?

Move #3: Moses sister, Miriam, had followed at a distance, just to see what good thing God would do, and now she rushed up to the Princess and said, "Do you know how to take care of a Jewish-boy-baby?

"Can't say that I do," answered the Daughter of the Kingdom. "Any ideas?"

"Oh, yes, I know just the lady," Miriam oozed. "I'll run and get her!"

She raced back to the slave hut, burst through the door and said, "Mother, you'll never guess what happened."

Jochebed replied, "Let me try. The ark was found in the bulrushes. Pharaoh's daughter had it brought to her. She opened the blanket and Moses began to cry. Not knowing what to do with a little baby like that . . . she sent you to get me. Pretty close?"

"That's exactly right. How did you know?"

"It just sounds like something God would do, Miriam. You need to learn that for yourself," Mother added.

They both went back to the spot where Moses and the Princess were waiting. Pharoah's daughter said, "You take this child and raise him until he is five years old . . . then bring him back to me. We'll send him to school and treat him like a king.

Babe in arms, Jochebed returned to the home that Moses had left only a few hours before . . . thinking all the way how good God is. And when we do our part . . . what great things we can expect Him to do.

Now there's the lesson for all of us. God does not ever do for us what we are expected to do for ourselves.

Prepare . . . prepare . . . prepare. Then get out of the way for God's extravagance.

As much as I hate to admit it . . . Dr. Reinhardt was right. Always pray, "God, bless me according to my preparation."

When you're ready . . . that's when He's ready.

And God will do the rest . . . best!

16

ALL OF THE CALL

He was barely a casual acquaintance, so I was a little surprised when he called saying he'd like to schedule time for a conference to get some counsel for his life. We had shared some seminars together in past meetings, so of course I was interested.

"What are we talking about?" was my first question.

"This has to do with my 'call'", he explained.

Well, if you know me, you know I'm always glad to talk . . . to anybody . . . anytime. We agreed on the hour and place and met face to face across a Coffee Shop table.

He began, "I'm quitting the ministry and I just wanted to give you my five reasons why."

Five reasons to quit the ministry? I could give you ten times more than that on the back of a napkin, if that's what you're looking for. It's never hard to find an excuse to escape anything, if you've been at it for a while. But I don't think stopping is the big question here. Starting is.

His approach bothered me. I couldn't help but say, "Before we get into the five reasons why you quit . . . how about giving me one good reason why you started."

You see, if you start for the wrong reason . . . you'll stop for the wrong reason.

I was invited out to a college to speak the other day . . . you always want to do your best at a college. They are such reservoirs of knowledge and erudition . . . at least it seems they certainly should be . . . especially when one considers how much learning the freshmen bring in with them and how little the seniors actually take away.

There was also the added disadvantage of being at my Alma Mater . . . I seem to get smarter the further I am from my roots. Five hundred miles is about the distance at which I begin to change into an absolute expert on any number of important topics and subjects.

So I studied hard . . . and prayed earnestly . . . because it is a deep challenge to speak to people that age. To try to add some direction to them from out here where I am . . . these thirty-some years from commencement. And to try to do so in a way that will not tarnish the brightness of their optimism. It is not a task that I take lightly.

I put on my best three-piece, dark, pin-stripe suit . . . thinking I would at least look like "a wise man from the east" and I went out to chapel and spoke. They were courteous and it seemed they listened attentively to me.

Afterward, I was down in front talking to some students, when someone looked down at my suit and said, "Well, look at THAT!" And I looked down to see what THAT was. My vest was buttoned wrong!

All the time I had been standing in front of those students thinking I was looking important, they must have been having a hard time paying attention to some guy who hadn't even passed Buttoning 101 yet.

It's really not hard to button your vest wrong . . . all you have to do is put the top button in the second hole. Or else slip the first hole over the second button. From then on it's as easy as falling off a log. Because the rest of them will follow along, slick as a whistle. All you have to do is start wrong. Ending wrong takes care of itself.

Always be careful to discern the difference between "calls" and "needs". There are many things that need to be done . . . but only a few things we are called of God to do.

Needs are everywhere . . . but Jesus never built His career or His ministry on needs. Of course He paused to help hurting people in their time of distress.

He fed the hungry . . . sometimes. But He knew they would need food again, so He never got into the FREE FOOD FOREVER business.

He healed the sick . . . sometimes. But they would have more physical needs in the days and years ahead . . . so He never set up a clinic to say, THIS IS WHY I CAME.

Of course all that is good to do . . . and it's needed! But Jesus never let the need overpower the call. He always knew who He was and why He was here.

Too often too many of us get our focus clouded. And it is focus that becomes the issue. Why are you doing what you're doing? That becomes the Life Question for all of us.

Capsulate it this way . . . never sacrifice the permanent on the altar of the immediate.

Lofty purpose is commendable . . . but it can sometimes be no more than simple presumption. Good motive (even towering aspiration) never guarantees proper resolution.

You learned it in Philosophy 101 . . . a false premise inevitably leads to a false conclusion.

Be sure you are responding to the CALL of the King

rather than the NEED of the near. Get that settled, all the rest happens naturally. My high school geometry teacher used to say, "You take care of the center . . . and the circumference will take care of itself."

And then understand all of the call. I Chronicles 29:5 puts the challenge like this: "Who then is willing to consecrate his service this day unto the Lord?"

This is a POINTED CALL. "Who then is WILLING . . ." More than once Jesus said, "He that hath ears to hear, let him hear." That does indicate that we can close out His voice and His call. But the faithful follower . . . never.

Now we're not talking volunteers here. This is servanthood. Did you ever notice how volunteers set their own schedule . . . they need affirmation and commendation . . . and they evade or avoid any duty that does not correspond with their agenda.

Servants, on the other hand, are always available . . . are open to any challenge . . . and are concerned only with their Master's call.

In II Corinthians 8:5 we read about the people who didn't just give offerings, but first gave their own selves. This call is pointedly personal.

Secondly, this is a PRECISE CALL. "Who then is willing to CONSECRATE . . ." Salvation, you know, is a gift . . . but consecration is a demand.

Did you ever notice that to most Christians, nouns are not the words that give us trouble. King, Lord, Saviour . . . all of those fit comfortably into our vocabulary. It's the verbs that disturb us. Forgive, go, deny, do . . . those mandates cause furrowed brows and furtive battles.

The demand of consecration is that all of our thanksgiving needs to be translated into thanksliving . . . every day.

A favorite practical preacher of mine used to enforce on us by his lifestyle the truth that Christianity is 2% theory . . . and 98% practice.

Sometimes the sheep don't need more feeding . . . they need more exercise. Otherwise we become as a mollycoddled engine, cleaned, polished, shiny and admired . . . but running nothing. Looking beautiful . . . but going no place.

In the third place this is a PERSONAL CALL . "Who then is willing to consecrate HIS SERVICE . . ." We begin by rejoicing in His love . . . we continue by engaging in His service.

When Dr. David Livingstone was working in Africa, a group of friends wrote him: "We would like to send other men to you. Have you found a good road into your area yet?"

Dr. Livingstone sent this message in reply: "If you have men who will only come if they know there is a good road, I don't want them. I want men who will come if there is no road at all."

God feels the same way. He doesn't need more men . . . He needs a better brand.

A Gypsy was standing at a fork in the road . . . tossing a stick into the air . . . and watching with great interest as it fell to the ground. And she kept on picking it up . . . tossing it high . . . looking at it drop . . . shaking her head . . . and then starting all over again.

After some time, a curious onlooker asked, "Just what are you doing?"

"I'm trying to get some direction on which way to travel," she answered. "At a fork in the road like this, my stick should tell me which way to go . . . right or left."

"But why do you keep throwing it in the air? Don't you have your answer yet?"

"I have to keep trying . . . it keeps coming down pointing left . . . and I want to go right! I'll keep throwing it till it works."

And lastly, this is a PRESSING CALL. "Who then is willing to consecrate his service THIS DAY to the Lord?"

Today . . . that's the key word. The plan of redemption is complete . . . now the world must be informed. And when do we do that? We start now . . . where we are . . . with what we have.

Today is never too soon.

In the Spring of 1967 a passenger express ran right up the back of a plodding freight train in Central California. Both trains were derailed and 36 lives were lost in the wreckage and flames.

During the investigation that followed, it was discovered that the automatic signaling system had been malfunctioning since early that day. One of the railroad employees was told to take a warning flag and station himself at the inoperative light to warn all engineers of impending traffic hazards.

Seeing the slow freight pass first . . . followed just a few minutes later by the speeding passenger express, the signal-man sensed the imminent disaster and frantically waved his flag.

The Judge asked the engineer, "Did you see the flag?"

"Yes, sir, I did," was the answer.

The Judge went further, "Why didn't you stop?"

"The flag was the wrong color, your Honor," the engineer replied.

The signal-man jumped up. "I waved the red flag. Anybody knows that means STOP!"

"It was a yellow flag meaning PROCEED SLOWLY WITH CAUTION."

"The flag was red!"

"The one we saw was yellow!"

The Judge's solution was simple. "Get the flag. We'll see for ourselves."

Guess what! Years ago the flag had been a bright red. But in the passage of time, the cloth had faded into a dull yellow. It had been so long since the flag had been used, no one even noticed.

One day a hen and a pig decided to honor their farmer friend. He had been a caring, faithful benefactor and now it was their turn to do something for him.

Said the hen, "I think we should do something extravagant."

Asked the pig, "Like what?"

The hen continued, "Like serve him breakfast in bed. How about a plateful of ham and eggs?"

Replied the pig, "Interesting you should suggest that combination . . . ham and eggs. For you that's involvement. For me . . . it's total commitment!"

17

TRANQUILIZED OR ENERGIZED

There are two views of life and two kinds of people. Some see life as a possession to be carefully guarded. They are SETTLERS. Others see life as a fantastic, wild explosive gift. They are PIONEERS.

The visible church is an outfit with an abundance of settlers and a few pioneers. The invisible church is the fellowship of pioneers.

To no one's surprise then, there are two kinds of theology. SETTLER THEOLOGY is an attempt to answer all the questions, define and housebreak some sort of "Supreme Being", establish the status quo on Golden Tablets in cinema scope.

PIONEER THEOLOGY is an attempt to talk about what it means to receive the strange gift of life and live it to the fullest. The pioneer sees theology as a wild adventure, complete with boisterous Indians, high risk and the haunting call of what is yet to be.

Settlers and Pioneers use the same words . . . but there the similarity ends.

THE CHURCH

In SETTLER THEOLOGY the church is the COURT-HOUSE. It is the center of town life. The old stone structure dominates the town square. Its windows are small. This makes the thing easy to defend, but quite dark inside. Its doors are solid oak. No one lives there except pigeons and they, of course, are most unwelcome.

Within the thick, courthouse walls records are kept, taxes collected, and trials are held for bad guys. The courthouse runs the town. It is the settler's symbol of law, order, stability, and most important, security. It is a society for the prevention of astonishment.

In PIONEER THEOLOGY the church is the COVERED WAGON. It is a house on wheels . . . always on the move. No place is its home. The covered wagon is where the pioneers eat, sleep, fight, love and die. It bears the marks of life and movement . . . it creaks, is scarred with arrows and bandaged with bailing wire. The covered wagon is always where the action is. It moves in on the future and doesn't bother to glorify its own ruts. The old wagon isn't comfortable, but the pioneers could care less. There is new territory to explore.

GOD

In SETTLER THEOLOGY God is the MAYOR, the honorable Alpha O. Mega, chief executive of Settler City. Dressed like a dude from back East, he lounges in an over-stuffed chair in this courthouse office. He keeps the blinds drawn. No one sees or knows him directly, but since there is law and order in the town, who can deny that he is there?

The MAYOR is predictable and always on schedule. He never does anything surprising or "out of the ordinary."

The settlers fear the MAYOR, but look to him to clear the payroll and keep things going. The MAYOR controls the courthouse which in turn runs the town. Peace and quiet are the MAYOR'S main concerns. That is why he sends the sheriff to check on pioneers who ride into town.

In PIONEER THEOLOGY God is the TRAIL BOSS. He is rough and rugged . . . full of life. The trail boss lives, eats, sleeps and fights alongside his men. Their well being is his concern. Without him the wagon wouldn't move . . . the pioneers would become fat and lazy. Living as free men would be impossible. The trail boss often gets down in the mud with the pioneers to help push the wagon which frequently gets stuck. He slugs the pioneers when they get soft and want to turn back. His fist is an expression of his concern.

JESUS

In SETTLER THEOLOGY Jesus is the SHERIFF. He is the guy who is sent by the mayor to enforce the rules. He wears a white hat, drinks milk, and outdraws the bad guys. He saves the settlers by offering security. The Sheriff decides who is thrown in jail. There is a saying in town that goes like this, "Those who believe the Mayor sent the Sheriff and follow the rules won't stay in boothill when it comes their time."

In PIONEER THEOLOGY Jesus is the SCOUT. He rides out ahead to find out which way the pioneers should go. He lives all the dangers of the trail. The scout suffers every hardship, is attacked by the Indians and is feared by the settlers. Through his actions and words he shows the true spirit, intent and concern of the Trail Boss. By looking at the Scout, those on the trail learn what it really means to be a pioneer.

THE HOLY SPIRIT

In SETTLER THEOLOGY the Holy Spirit is a SALOON GIRL. Her job is to comfort the settlers. They come to her when they feel lonely, or when life gets dull or dangerous. She tickles them under the chin and makes everything O.K. again. The Saloon Girl squeals to the Sheriff when someone starts disturbing the peace. (Note to settlers: The whiskey served in Settler City Saloon is the nonalcoholic kind.)

In PIONEER THEOLOGY the Holy Spirit is the BUFFALO HUNTER. He rides along with the wagon train and furnishes fresh, raw meat for the pioneers. Without it they would die. The buffalo hunter is a strange character . . . sort of a wild man. The pioneers never can tell what he will do next. He scares the hell out of the settlers. He has a big, black gun that goes off like a cannon. He amuses himself by riding into town on Sunday to shake up the settlers, who have a little ice cream party in the courthouse every Sunday morning. With his gun in hand the buffalo hunter sneaks up to one of the courthouse windows and fires a tremendous blast which shakes the entire courthouse. Men jump out of their skin, women scream and dogs bark. Chuckling to himself, the buffalo hunter rides back to the wagon train shooting up the town as he goes.

THE CHRISTIAN

In SETTLER THEOLOGY the Christian is the SET-TLER. He fears the open, unknown frontier. His concern is to stay in good with the Mayor and keep out of the Sheriff's way. He tends a small garden. "Safety First" is his motto. To him the courthouse is a symbol of security, peace, order and happiness. He keeps his money in the bank. The banker is his best friend. He spends his time playing checkers in the restful shade of the oak trees lining the courthouse lawn. He never misses an ice cream party.

In PIONEER THEOLOGY the Christian is the PIO-NEER. He is a man of risk and daring . . . hungry for adventure, new life and the challenge of the journey. He is tough, rides hard and knows how to use a gun when necessary. The pioneer feels sorry for the town folks and tries to tell them about the joy and fulfillment of a life following the trail. He dies with his boots on.

THE CLERGYMAN

In SETTLER THEOLOGY the Clergyman is the BANKER. Within his vaults are locked the values of the town. He is suspicious of strangers. And why not? Look what he has to protect! The Banker is a highly respected man in town. He has a gun but keeps it hidden behind a book in his middle desk drawer. He feels that he and the Sheriff have a lot in common. After all, they both protect the bank.

In PIONEER THEOLOGY the Clergyman is the COOK. He doesn't furnish the meat . . . he just dishes up what the buffalo hunter provides. This is how he supports the movement of the wagon. He never confuses his job with the job of the Trail Boss, Scout or Buffalo Hunter. He sees himself as just another pioneer who has learned to cook. The cook's job is to help the pioneers pioneer.

FAITH

In SETTLER THEOLOGY faith is trusting in the safety of the Town. It is obeying the laws, keeping your nose clean, believing the mayor is in the courthouse.

In PIONEER THEOLOGY faith is the spirit of adventure. It is the readiness to move out, to risk everything on the trail, to obey to the restless voice of the Trail Boss.

SIN

In SETTLER THEOLOGY sin is breaking one of the Town's ordinances.

In PIONEER THEOLOGY sin is wanting to turn back.

SALVATION

In SETTLER THEOLOGY salvation is living close to home and hanging around the Courthouse.

In PIONEER THEOLOGY salvation is being more afraid of sterile town life than death on the trail, joy at the thought of another day to push on into the unknown, trusting the Trail Boss, following the Scout, living on the meat provided by the Buffalo Hunter.

THE TRINITY

In SETTLER THEOLOGY the Trinity is viewed like this:
The Mayor makes the laws.
The Sheriff enforces them.
The Saloon Girl helps people forget their troubles.

In PIONEER THEOLOGY the Trinity is viewed like this:
The Trail Boss built the wagon and keeps it moving.
The Scout reveals the purpose of the Trail Boss.
The Buffalo hunter furnishes meat to sustain the drive.

JOIN UP . . . MOVE OUT . . . CARRY ON!

18

NO ONE SAYS YOUR NAME LIKE JESUS

It was my turn to visit Miss Emily. The Pastoral Staff took turns driving the 19 miles out of town to her "spread". She was 83 years old and had always lived alone . . . except for her "critters" . . . a strange array of cats, dogs, goats and varmints.

Someone made a weekly call (mine were weakly) to check up on her and try to talk her into leaving the country and becoming more like city folks. Pastor Butcher didn't care when in the week the call was made . . . just as long as it was done before Sunday. I always waited as long as possible . . . at least until Friday afternoon. I knew that if Jesus returned, I wouldn't have to brave the journey.

It wasn't the trip that was bad . . . it was the atmosphere. We're talking ripe . . . really ripe! I'd get to the front gate and then wait in my car for a few minutes gaining courage for the pilgrimage across the yard and up on to the porch. Success was getting there without falling through or stepping in anything.

On this day . . . I made it unscathed. She met me at the door saying, "I thought you'd never get here."

"One can only hope," I thought . . . but I said, "Lots of nice animals today." (I don't know why I said it . . . I just did.)

"Yep," she replied. "Some are nice and some are not, and it's always fun watching people figure out who is which." (I like to make people happy . . . and if that's what it took for her . . . she should have been as cheerful as a bald headed bumblebee in a field of red clover.)

We sat down to chat for a while and there was a bowl of peanuts on the coffee table. As the two of us chatted, I kept nibbling at those nuts one at a time and, without realizing it, ate them all. With some embarrassment I apologized for my intemperance, explaining that I had been so into the conversation that I'd not even noticed what I was doing.

"Oh, that's all right," Miss Emily assured me. "My teeth are so bad that I can't eat the peanuts anyway. I just lick off the chocolate and drop the nuts in that old bowl."

At that point I asked if there were anything I could do for her and without hesitation she blurted out, "Yes. I have some mail here that someone needs to read for me. I sat on my glasses three weeks ago and the letters are piling up."

She pointed to an old dresser and I opened the top drawer. Inside were twenty-two envelopes . . . but to my shock and dismay, every one of them was addressed to OCCUPANT or RESIDENT.

No one knew her name.

You can be sure that I made up letters to read that day. She was purring happy (just like her cats) when I left her outpost. But my heart was hurting over that forgotten lady.

And then it dawned on me. She wasn't really forgotten. There was Someone Who knew her name. Remember what He said, "My sheep know my voice, and I call them by name."

And no one says your name like Jesus.

Remember Mary? Sitting all alone in the garden . . . just

crying. The tomb was empty . . . and Jesus was gone. He had been the only true friend she had. All of her life people had ignored her or looked down on her because of who she was and what she did. But not Him. He acted like He really cared. And now He was gone . . . and her promise of life gone with Him.

She was lost in her tears and didn't pay any attention to the man who walked up behind her. She simply supposed that he was the gardener . . . until He softly said, "Mary." She knew that voice. It had to be Jesus . . . because no one ever said her name like He did.

Zacchaeus had met Jesus once before at the dinner Matthew had hosted when he renounced his old life of tax collecting. And when Zacchaeus heard that Jesus was coming through Jericho today, he wanted to see him again.

But Zacchaeus was faced with a three fold problem. He had a moral handicap in that he was a publican and had achieved his livelihood dishonestly. He had a social handicap, for he was rich, and Jesus said it was harder for a rich man to enter into heaven than for a camel to go through a needle's eye.

Added to this was a physical handicap which further impeded his progress. He was small of stature and could not see Jesus because of the crowd that thronged Him. But the little man did not give up. He overcame his limitations by running ahead of the people and climbing a sycamore tree to get a better look at the passing Saviour.

What Zacchaeus lacked in legs he made up in will power. And after all, it isn't the length of the legs that counts, but how fast you can move them. A jack rabbit can outrun a horse if it wants to.

God plants trees. But we must choose to climb them. And now Jesus was standing under that sycamore, looking up, calling him by name . . . "Zacchaeus, come down. Today . . . I'll have dinner at your house." No one said his name like He did.

Lazarus had already been in the grave for three days when Jesus got there. Mary and Martha were upset at His delay and said, "You can't do anything now . . it's too late!" But Jesus said, "If you believe then you shall see the glory of God." And then He called His friend, "Lazarus . . . Lazarus, come forth!" and not even death could not hold him back when Jesus said his name.

One time Jesus sent seventy disciples out over the country side to share the good news that they had received. When those disciples returned from the tour of ministry all excited about their miracles and healings, Jesus reminded them, "As wonderful as that is . . . there is something greater. Rejoice rather, that your names are written in the Lamb's Book of Life."

Jim had just become a believer and was new to the faith. Someone had encouraged him to get into a church and begin sharing the fellowship. He discovered a sanctuary that was open for prayer during the day, and decided that would be a good place to start. He knew his weekends would be taken care of and, like a Dachshund, he felt he could use support in the middle.

So every day he left work at noon and found his way to the altar of his church. He never stayed long . . . not more than 30 or 40 seconds. And that caught the Pastor's eye. It seemed like an inordinately short time for prayer. But he noticed that Jim kept coming . . . as sure as Tuesday followed Monday.

After a few weeks of this habit, my Pastor friend stopped Jim on the way out one noon and asked, "What in the world do you pray about for 45 seconds that would make it worth your while to come in here every day?"

Jim thought for a moment as if puzzled . . . and then he smiled. "I never considered that before. I guess I just come to say, 'Jesus, it's Jim.' That's plenty to remind me that I have a Heavenly Father to live for and enough for Him to notice that He has a little boy down here to look out after."

Every day Jim kept coming. He'd bow at the altar and pray his simple prayer, "Jesus, it's Jim," and then wait a moment, as if for confirmation the message had been received, then get up and head back for the office.

Rain or shine, hot or cold, in busy season or slack, it was always the same. The weeks passed into months and the months into years. He was there to nod at his Pastor, to kneel in prayer and to open his heart with, "Jesus, it's Jim."

Then one night at 2:30 the parsonage phone rang. It was Jim's wife. There had been a terrible accident. Would the Pastor come to the hospital . . . and please hurry.

He dressed quickly and took the 15 minute drive consumed in his own prayer for this special friend. When he walked into the emergency room no one needed to say anything about how serious this was. One look at Jim was all it took.

The Pastor glanced consolingly at the family and then bent over the bed. Jim looked at him through half glazed eyes. "It won't be long," the Pastor thought to himself, then spoke softly, "Jim. We may not have much more time together. I need to know . . . are you ready to go?"

Jim barely moved his lips.

Through his tears the Pastor tried again, "Jim. This is really important. When you step into the next life, are you prepared to meet Him?"

Jim looked up at his friend said, "Do you remember all the times I came and prayed, 'Jesus, it's Jim?'"

The Pastor nodded. He remembered well.

Jim smiled past his pain. "I just heard a voice. You know what it said? 'Jim . . . it's Jesus.'"

19

THE RULES

You know that our legislators have enacted over 10,000,000 laws to enforce the Ten Commandments. We are indeed a populace of rules and regulations. And most of them smite the olfactory senses right where it hurts. Like the sign on the perfume counter reminded us last busy Christmas season:

OUT OF ODOR.

How about these for a new look at Crime Time? They all are (or once were) real laws. Can you believe it is a crime . . .

... to bathe less than once a year in Kentucky, and more than once a week in Boston.
... to catch mice in Cleveland without a hunting license.
... to tie a giraffe to a telephone pole in Atlanta.
... to whistle underwater in Vermont.
... to put a skunk in your boss's desk in Michigan.
... to own a copy of THE ENCYCLOPEDIA BRITANNICA in Texas because it contains a liquor recipe.

. . . to get a fish drunk anywhere in the state of Oklahoma.

. . . to go to church in Georgia without a loaded rifle.

. . . to give your sweetheart in Idaho a box of candy weighing less than 50 pounds.

. . . to eat a snake on Sunday anywhere in Kansas.

. . . to eat in a place that is on fire in Chicago.

. . . to go to bed with your boots on in North Dakota.

. . . to ride in a baby carriage in Roderfield, West Virginia, unless you are a baby.

AND: Whenever two trains meet at a crossing in Texas, both of them must come to a full stop. Then neither one may proceed until the other has gone.

Where ever you go, what ever you do . . . it seems that someone will have a better idea about ordering conduct and organizing performance. Just the other day I found this list on the bulletin board at the EPCOT Entertainment Office.

THE RULES

1. The female always makes The Rules.
2. The Rules are subject to change at any time without prior notification.
3. No male can possibly know all The Rules.
4. If the female suspects the male knows all The Rules, she must immediately change some or all of The Rules.
5. The female is never wrong.
6. If the female is wrong, it is because of a flagrant misunderstanding, which was a direct result of something the male did or said wrong.
7. If The Rule #6 applies, the male must apologize immediately for causing the misunderstanding.

8. The female can change her mind at any given point in time.
9. The male must never change his mind without express written consent from the female.
10. The female has every right to be angry or upset at any time.
11. The male must remain calm at all times, unless the female wants him to be angry or upset.
12. The female must under no circumstances let the male know whether or not she wants him to be angry or upset.
13. If the female has PMS all The Rules are null and void!

Yep . . . rules are everywhere. The other day I even heard some friends disagreeing (arguing, to be exact) about how to pray. You know, proper praying posture, verbal exactness, prioritizing the order of requests. Wow. What ever happened to the simple speaking to God . . . like when Peter was sinking in The Sea of Galilee and cried, "Lord, save me!" Pretty short, pretty spontaneous, pretty effective.

And when Elijah prayed for the fire to fall in I Kings 18:36-37, his prayer was only 63 words long (33 in the original Hebrew) and takes less than a minute to complete! But the result lasted for a life time . . . and more.

So I did a little research. What is the best way to pray? Standing up, sitting down or kneeling? Well, actually any of those three postures are equally authorized according to Scripture. And did you know there are 17 other acceptable ways?

You can pray while lying prostrate or with raised hands,
silently or aloud,
alone or together,
at fixed times or any time.

How about everywhere?
    In bed.
        In the fields.
            In the temple.
                At the riverside.
                    At the seashore.
                        On the battlefield.
                            Spontaneously or liturgically.

So it doesn't seem to matter to God what our physical prayer position is. In fact . . . listen to this:

"The proper way for a man to pray,"
  Said Deacon Lemuel Keys,
"The only proper attitude
  Is down upon your knees."

"No, I should say the way to pray,"
  Said Reverend Doctor Wise,
"Is standing straight with outstretched arms
  And rapturous upturned eyes."

"It seems to me his hands should be
  Devoutly clasped in front,
With both thumbs pointing toward the ground,"
  Said Reverend Doctor Blunt.

"Last year I fell in Hopkins' well,
  Head first," said Cyrus Brown,
"With both my heels a stickin' up,
  And my head a-pointin' down.

"And I made a prayer right then and there;
  Best prayer I ever said.
The prayin'est I ever prayed
  Was standin' on my head!!"

So you see, there are times it doesn't matter HOW we pray, just that we DO. But always pray with sincerity. When I repeat the Lord's Prayer, I cannot say OUR if I live in a logic-tight spiritual compartment thinking only people who agree with me are going to heaven.

I cannot say FATHER if I do not demonstrate that relationship in my daily life.

I cannot say WHICH ART IN HEAVEN if I am so occupied with the earth that I am laying up no treasure there.

I cannot say HALLOWED BE THY NAME if I, who am called by His name, am not holy.

I cannot say THY WILL BE DONE if I am questioning, resentful or disobedient to His will for me.

I cannot say ON EARTH AS IT IS IN HEAVEN if I am not prepared to devote my life here to His service.

I cannot say GIVE US THIS DAY OUR DAILY BREAD if I am living on past experience, or looking elsewhere for satisfaction and motivation.

I cannot say FORGIVE US OUR TRESPASSES AS WE FORGIVE THOSE THAT TRESPASS AGAINST US if I harbor a grudge against anyone.

I cannot say LEAD US NOT INTO TEMPTATION if I deliberately place myself or remain in a position where I am likely to be tempted.

I cannot say DELIVER US FROM EVIL if I am not prepared to fight it in the spiritual realm with the weapon of prayer.

I cannot say THINE IS THE KINGDOM if I do not accord the King the disciplined obedience of a loyal subject.

I cannot say THINE IS THE POWER if I fear what men may do or what my neighbors may think.

I cannot say THINE IS THE GLORY if I am seeking glory for myself.

I cannot say FOR EVER AND EVER if my horizon is bounded by the things of time.

I cannot say AMEN if I do not also add the phrase "cost what it may." Because to say this prayer honestly will take everything I have.

God never has altered the rules to fit the man . . .
. . . but always the man to fit the rules.

20

THE NIGHT GOD CRIED

It's a late evening in North Israel. In a humble home there a lonely figure sits sobbing, head buried in his hands. A loved one has left the home, and the bereaved husband is holding a funeral in his heart.

Why had it all happened? This is the question that haunts the mind and harrows the soul of the young prophet, Hosea.

Memory takes him by the hand and leads him back across the trail of the years. How vividly he recalls the time when he first met the beautiful girl named Gomer. The scene shapes itself again before his eyes. The charm of youth, her entrancing loveliness . . . the recollections of that hour stir and stab his heart this night.

Conscious of his calling, the young prophet had prayed earnestly about the matter. Clear as the notes of a bell the divine directive had come: "Marry Gomer." And so they had been joined in wedlock. In spite of all the tragedy that had followed, Hosea could not doubt that God had instructed him to marry the one who became his wife. But why? Why? The question resounded like a scream through his soul.

Those first years had been such happy ones! Hosea was

very affectionate by nature, and his young bride had loved him as he loved her. As the fragrance of lilacs in May, so the breezes of memory carried a scent of the sweetness of those early days

Well did he remember the first child he held in his arms. The proud father of a son, it seemed that his cup of joy was full. As the prophet prayed he was instructed to call the boy's name "Jezreel." The little lad was to be a sign to the nation that God would avenge the blood of Jezreel upon the house Jehu.

But then a little rift seemed to be entering their happy marriage. Hosea noted with growing concern the increasing attention shown his young wife by other men. Quick looks and coy glances exchanged messages that his eyes sometimes intercepted. It was not difficult to decode them. Gomer's very beauty was proving a snare to her. Tragedy was lurking just around the corner, looking on with greedy eyes. Gentle persuasion proved unavailing. The only thing the prophet could do was to pray.

After a while a second child was born into the home ... this time a daughter. It was not the fact that it was a girl rather than a boy that cooled Hosea's enthusiasm. Over the scene there lay the dark shadow of an awful uncertainty. Was this child really his own? Hosea's horizon was filled with a haunting question mark.

There was little comfort in the name assigned this child by the divine voice "Call her name Lo-ruhamah: for I will no more have mercy on the house of Israel". Lo-ruhamah. Unloved. Unpitied.

Daily tragedy was stalking the young prophet's footsteps, leering at him from behind every passing incident. Slowly the burden was being laid upon his shoulders . . . the hidden burden of a harrowing fear.

Finally a third child was born. This time there was no question mark . . . only a horrible certainty. God said: "Call his name Lo-ammi: for ye are not my people, and I will not be your God." Lo-ammi . . . "not my people, no kin of mine."

Stunned and dazed, Hosea walked about as if he were in a dream. The sensitive soul of the prophet was bombarded with all the stark reality of the terrible truth. The child was not his own. His wife, Gomer, had been untrue to him. She had left his love for another's lust.

What should he do? That had been the problem that perplexed the prophet. Deep down in his heart, love for his wife burned with unquenchable flame. He could not bear to think of putting her away. But as a man of God he could not live in companionship with sin. There was only one course he could take.

Frankly he placed the issue squarely before Gomer. Tenderly he pled with her for the last time. Would she turn her back on her false lovers and be true to him?

While the children's voices floated into the room from their play outside, husband and wife sat facing each other in the little home. With a breaking heart Hosea looked into the face of the woman whom he loved.

Like a drowning man grasping for a straw he searched her face for just one sign of penitence and answering love. And as he waited trembling and afraid, she lifted her eyes to his for just one brief moment.

But the look he saw there was to stab his heart again and again in the days that followed. It was not repentance but rebellion that he saw there. It was a look of stubbornness and self-will.

"Gomer," he breathed, "will you? Won't you, Gomer?" A moment of silence. Then a hoarse whisper, "No."

Crushed with a grief which pressed his heart with almost unendurable pain, the prophet buried his face and sought to hold back the tears. As if from a distance he heard his wife move about the house gathering a few things to take with her.

Then he heard her open the door. An overpowering impulse swept through his being. He must take her in his arms, hold her fast, tell her his love, not let her go. But no. Love to be pure must be true.

Finally he heard her footsteps fade away down the road. An awful sense of empty loneliness crept over the prophet's spirit. It seemed that the light of love had gone out in his soul.

And then the dams burst, and Hosea found relief in a rushing torrent of hot tears.

In just a minute the children came hurrying in. "Where is Mamma going? She didn't answer us when we called her. Why did she leave?" Yes ... why? Hosea had no answer.

That evening a strange silence pervaded the supper hour. Everyone was conscious of the empty place in the family circle. Suddenly little Lo-ruhamah looked up into his face. "Where's Mamma tonight?"

Like the quick stab of a cruel knife the question struck home. Hosea tried to choke back the tears. He could only shake his head. Lo-ruhamah moved up close to him and started to cry. Over and over she moaned, "I want my Mamma. I want my Mamma." The prophet leaned his head down close to hers, and they wept together. He wanted her, too.

But he realized he must not give way before the children. Quietly he gathered them around for evening prayers. With faltering lips he uttered the prayer which welled up within him, "Take care of Mamma tonight ... where ever she is ... and bring her home safe ... and soon."

With the children tucked in safely for the night, Hosea turned his attention to putting the house in order. Now the little ones were all tucked in bed, sleeping soundly. In the opposite corner of the one-room house Hosea threw himself on his face and gave way to his grief.

With only God to listen, he sobbed out the sorrow of his soul. Anguish passed into agony and out of the darkness of his despair he cried, "O God, why?"

The answer came in an unexpected way. Worn out with weeping the prophet became quiet for a moment. In that silent pause he heard a sound. Startled, he lifted his head. No . . . the children were all breathing regularly in a deep sleep.

Once more he buried his head in his arms. Then he heard it again. Someone was sobbing . . . someone besides himself. It was not the children. Who could it be?

Breathlessly he waited in perfect silence. Then it came once more. This time he caught some words . . . listen! "How shall I give thee up, Ephraim? O Ephraim, what shall I do unto thee? How, oh how shall I give thee up?" It was the sob of a broken hearted God.

That night Hosea learned that he did not suffer alone. At the heart of the universe was a God of love who was sorrowing over the sins of His people. As Gomer had been untrue to her husband, so Israel had been untrue to her God. In the fellowship of suffering Hosea had found a new message for the nation. Israel's greatest sin was that of rejecting God's love. But God, though His love is spurned, loves still.

One night a few months later as the prophet was praying, the Voice spoke clearly again in his soul. "Go yet, love a woman beloved of her friend, yet an adulteress, according to the love of the Lord toward the children of Israel."

The next morning Hosea sent the children out to play with their neighbors. Then he walked down that same road which Gomer had followed some months before. It led from their quiet, country home toward Bethel a few miles away.

As Hosea entered the streets of that big city, he noticed the same sights and sounds which had shocked Amos only a few years before. While the thin veneer of prosperity was breaking off in some spots, many people still lived in luxury and ease.

Down through the better part of the city Hosea went, until he came to the slum section. All that he saw now was new to him. He had never visited the place before.

He noticed a large crowd, walked that direction and then recognized the place as the slave market.

As he drew near, his attention was drawn to one slave especially. She was dressed in filthy rags, yet something about her looked strangely familiar.

Just then she turned her face his way. Their eyes met . . . just for one moment. Then she looked quickly the other way. But in that brief glance Hosea had caught a glimmer of recognition. It hardly seemed possible, but it was true. The slave was Gomer!

With his heart beating fast, Hosea bargained with the owner. "So I bought her to me for fifteen pieces of silver, and for an homer of barley, and half homer of barley."

As the prophet stepped forward to take his purchase, the once beautiful young woman hung her head in shame. She had sold herself as a slave to sin, and now she found herself helpless in literal slavery. But her husband was redeeming her.

Lovingly Hosea took her hand, and together they walked back past the slums and through the better section and finally out into the open country on the road toward home.

Not a word had yet been spoken. Then tenderly, gently, came words that started earthquake tremors in Gomer's soul. Softly the one beside her said, "Gomer... I love you. My heart has never lost its love. Every day, every night I have longed for you and prayed for you. Not once have I given you up. Now I have bought you back to be my own forever. All the past is forgiven. You must stay with me and never be untrue to me again. We will set up a new home, a happy home, and be true to each other as long as we live."

Blinded by tears, Gomer stumbled along beside her husband. Soon they were approaching the little home that had been and was to be theirs.

How good it looked now, compared with the miserable hovels of sin and the awful slave market! Hosea opened the door and gently ushered her in.

When Gomer found herself in her own home with her husband again, an overwhelming sense of the awfulness of sin swept over her. She saw herself as she really was, and hated her sinful self with a passionate abhorrence.

Falling on her knees she poured out her heart in confession and contrition. With sobs and groans she pleaded for forgiveness. it didn't seem possible that God could forgive. But Hosea had. Maybe God would.

Suddenly the light of heaven broke into her sin-darkened heart. She looked up with a radiant smile shining through her tears. Hosea clasped her in his arms. Once more she was really his bride. Love had found a way. The prodigal wife had come home.

Out of this home-made tragedy in Hosea's life comes the greatest message of the Bible, the story of God's redeeming love. Amos had thundered in tones of stern justice. Hosea uttered it in tones of tender love.

Why the difference? The heartache and heartbreak that came to the prophet who lost his loved one to sin . . . and then bought her back again. The passionate pleading of Hosea's ministry is but an echo of the sob he heard that night in the dark.

Ben was nine years old and spent all his summer spare time building his pride-and-joy-sailboat. It was a beautiful sight to behold . . . smooth hull, hand-formed lead keel, and the bleached-sheet-turned-sails billowing in the wind.

Ben would watch his boat head out across the pond. He'd chase it to the other side . . . walk it back and start her out again.

On the third day of sailing somehow she went astray. Contrary wind? Curious current? Ben never did know . . . but he knew he lost her. He searched for the best part of the next week. Never could find her.

He cried himself to sleep more than one night because of loneliness and despair. What do you do when that which you love the most slides out of your life? Ben couldn't come up with an answer. He felt so betrayed.

Then walking through town, he stopped at a toy shop. There in the window was his sailboat! It was easy to recognize . . . his markings were everywhere. Inside the store he told the shopkeeper that he wanted the boat back.

"Sorry," said the owner. "That boat is mine. I bought it from a boy who found it last week. If you want it . . . you'll have to pay for it."

"Please keep the boat till I get back," he asked.

Ben raced home . . . gathered all his resources . . . and

zipped back to the store. He plunked down the full price, picked up his ship and walked out the door saying, "Oh, little boat. Now you are twice mine. First I made you . . . then I bought you. Now . . . forever . . . you really do belong to me!"

21

LIFETIME QUESTIONS

Tell someone there are 4 billion stars in the universe, and he'll believe you. But hang up a WET PAINT sign, and he has to test it for himself to be sure it's true.

Why are goods sent by ship called cargo, while commodities sent in a car are a shipment?

How can it be true that quicksand works slowly?

And that boxing rings are square?

And that public bathrooms have no baths?

We are raised to question and wonder. There are inquiries on every hand:

How can you make amends . . . but not just one amend? Can you comb through the annals of history for just one annal? And if you have a bunch of odds and ends, and you get rid of all but one, what do you call it?

How can my house burn up at the same time it burns down? How do I fill in a form by filling it out? And how can my alarm clock go off by going on?

Did you know that the simple question, "Can You Please Help Me?" has turned into big business. Encyclopedias have

set up assistance divisions, major corporations offer 24 hour diagnostic service by phone for their products and appliances. And the New York Public Library has answered 6.2 million questions over the past two decades? Yep . . . hot items like
. . .

WHAT DOES "KEMO SABE" MEAN?

As used by Tonto toward the Lone Ranger, it was intended to mean "faithful friend." But in Navaho it means "soggy bush."

WHO PUT THE "TOOTSIE" IN TOOTSIE ROLLS?

Candy maker Leo Hirschfield created and marketed a new sweet treat in 1896, calling it Tootsie Rolls, the pet name for his daughter, Clara.

WHO WAS THE MOST MARRIED MAN IN HISTORY?

Mongkut of Siam . . . the king in THE KING AND I . . . who had 9,000 wives and concubines, beating out Solomon by more than a few.

WHY DO MEN BUTTON FROM THE RIGHT AND WOMEN FROM THE LEFT?

In the past men usually dressed themselves, and because most men are right-handed, buttoning up from that side was easier. But ladies were dressed by maids who found it more convenient to work from the lady's left.

To me, questions are a big part of what makes the world-go-round. There is something joyous about the quest . . . the problem and the solution.

When I was approaching my senior year in college, it

became apparent that I better find out what the rest of my life was about. I couldn't, shouldn't and wouldn't be a college student all of my life. I was barely existing in that category now. All the world was waiting for me . . . and I knew that I could reach as far as my dreams could take me.

That got me to my first big question for life . . . WHAT? If this really was the first day of the rest of my life, what was I going to do? What? WHAT? WHAT?

I started with "What would I do if I knew I couldn't fail?" Now that offered some incredible possibilities. Of course it had to be matched with the sub-question, "Is there any reason you might or should fail?" It is important that realism take some part in this hope-dream picture. (Obviously, given my bodily frame and weight handicap, there were about 200 pounds of good reason that I could never be a jockey on a Kentucky Derby winner.)

And then I moved on to "What would I like to be remembered as?" You know, when I'm gone, what will people say about me? Think about me? Cherish about me? And . . . what am I doing now to create the memory?

After getting some definition on WHAT, there was the next big question . . . HOW? How am I going to make this dream come true. The geographic location, the definition of personal abilities, the opportunities to grow, as well as who I would share the possibilities with, all entered into the equation.

Three ingredients are essential to succeed in any endeavor. They are MOTIVATION, ABILITY and OPPORTUNITY. And they must appear in basically equal proportions.

Two will never cut it. How many people do you know who

have MOTIVATION and OPPORTUNITY . . . but no ABILITY. They'll never make it.

And others with OPPORTUNITY and ABILITY . . . but no MOTIVATION. Just plain lazy . . . not a chance.

Unfortunately, there are some with ABILITY and MOTIVATION . . . but not OPPORTUNITY. Out-a-here! It absolutely takes all three. A dream alone is not enough.

I tried my skills and enthusiasm in one position for a while and truly had a great time. Then things began to turn in on me. Sizzle was being replaced by stress, activity was becoming more important than accomplishment, and joy was overtaken by job.

So there I was . . . face to face with my Life Question #3: WHY? And here's where we start to get to the nitty-gritty of it all. WHY . . . that's the focus question. WHAT and HOW are secular and earthly questions. They must be answered . . . or else things are not done decently and in order. This third question brings to light our motivation and ministry emphasis. It is the Jesus Question. WHAT you're doing and HOW you'll do it are yours to answer. But WHY . . . that's where you face Him.

Then, after you've solved the WHAT, HOW and WHY questions, you run into the next big one . . . WHO CARES? You work long and hard, covering yourself with sweat, fatigue and confusion, only to discover that no one seems to care. At least not as far as the job description is concerned.

Maybe only God cares . . . and you remember the final score is not being kept down here anyway.

Maybe only you notice. Some things you do just to prove

to yourself that you can really do it. (God already knows you can . . . so it's just for you.) But in whatever you do . . . be sure that there is someone who cares.

And here's a biggy . . . WHAT NEXT? You've always got to be looking and planning, checking the opportunities and options. Orval Butcher, my main ministry mentor, was always asking, "What's your encore?" By that he meant, "I know everything is under control for this event, project or endeavor. But what happens next?"

To him, creativity was like a bicycle ride. To be working on one project at a time was the same as pedaling a one-pedaled bike up a hill. Push that one pedal down and then you spend most of the rest of your time sticking your foot under the pedal to pull it back up again so you can shove it down to keep going forward. Trouble is . . . you lose all your momentum . . . and are probably ready to fall off.

Two concepts were like two pedals . . . not just nice, but necessary. It kept everyone motivated and thinking ahead. It instilled excitement and encouraged inspiration. It was Pastor Butcher's clarion call to excellence . . . "What's your encore?"

And then there's one more question we need to face. When Walt Disney decided to proceed with his new concept of a theme park in Anaheim, California, he told his staff, "I know who we need to be the chief construction engineer."

The immediate staff response was, "Who? Tell us who and we'll get him right away."

"I don't know his name . . . but I do know who he is. Whoever put the United States Navy back in the war in 1942 is the man I want. Find him," was the Disney declaration.

(For those of you who missed it, we lost most of our fleet in the early days of December 1941 at the beginning of World War II, and someone had masterminded the effort to make us competitive. By the end of the year 1942 we were afloat again, sailing into the Pacific, and winning the war.)

The staff discovered the champion of that naval cause was Joe Fowler. Admiral Joe Fowler, fifty years old and retiring from the Service. At first he declined the Disney invitation because he couldn't stand California and he hated mice. But he reconsidered to get the expense paid trip and time with his wife in exchange for one afternoon's listening to a foolhardy dream.

But it only took that one afternoon in 1952 to catch the imagination and steal the heart of the Admiral . . . and he signed on for the project. He was the chief construction engineer for the twenty-five million dollar job.

Twenty years later when Walt Disney wanted to open a sister theme park in Florida, retired Admiral Joe Fowler again was the boss of it all. A one hundred million dollar investment being managed by a 70 year old man.

Ten years later . . . when EPCOT Center was planned on the Disney World property in Florida, guess who the chief construction engineer was. You're right . . . 80 year old Joe Fowler! Managing a project that would cost a thousand million dollars . . . that's a billion with a "B"! Eighty years old . . . this is the man who said, "You don't have to die until you're ready to die!" You understand that? If you have a dream . . . you can keep on going. Never, never stop stretching your soul.

What made Walt Disney so secure in the leadership of Joe Fowler? Let this incident open the door of your understanding.

If you have visited Disneyland in California, then you have seen the Pirates of the Caribbean, a white-knuckle ride down two waterfalls and then an exciting cruise through a pirate battle.

The day before the ride was to open, Walt Disney took his usual preview tour. "This show can't open like this. It's not ready."

The staff replied, "Ready? Of course it's ready! Everything is up to specifications and all the inspections are completed and passed."

"It's still not ready," he insisted. "We have a bayou restaurant here and no fire-flies. It is impossible to have a bayou property without lightning bugs!"

"What do you want us to do about that?" came the quick question.

"I don't have any idea," Walt said. "Call Joe. He'll know."

When Joe was contacted, he only had one question. Not "how many does he want?" or "how shall we suspend them?" or "does he want incandescent, florescent, or reflective light?"

None of those.

Walt Disney wants fire-flies? Joe Fowler asked only one question . . . WHEN?"

And I think that's the question for all of us. We all know what we ought to be and how we ought to be it. The knowing is not the problem.

It's the WHEN . . . WHEN shall we be what we are intended to be and when do we do what we are designed to do?

I vote for now!

22

RISK IT

"Take care!" I hear it all the time. You do, too. Walking out of offices. Exiting restaurants. Even leaving Church.

And that's the absolutely worst thing any one believer could say to another believer. Where is the encouragement to reach, hope, trust or achieve?

Imagine God leaning over the balcony of heaven, looking down at His Son lying in a manger and saying, "Now Jesus, be careful. Don't do anything to get in trouble down there. Just say some nice things that people can write down and remember for a future day. You might want to feed some hungry people and it would be nice to help some needy people get well. You could even perform a few miracles . . . You know . . . blind people see, lame people walk. Any thing like that would be more than wonderful. I'll check back in thirty-three years and see how it's gone for You. But above all, Son Jesus . . . do be careful!!"

A cosmic conversation like that is hard to imagine let alone believe! What God really said was, "Jesus . . . risk it! Go for it all. What ever it takes to redeem mankind . . . RISK IT!!"

And likewise to us . . . God always says the same thing.

Remember how Paul phrased it for Him? "Be careful for . . . NOTHING!" Risk it! And the words of Jesus Himself: "All things are possible!"

The Gospel of Mark is full of faith-risks.

Chapter 2: Four men bring a crippled friend to a house in Capernaum where Jesus is preaching. The crowd is so large there is no room to get in the door. Check verse 4 . . . "when they could not". . . they found a way anyway! That's how to risk.

Chapter 3: The man with the withered hand sitting in the back shadows of the Capernaum synagogue. Jesus told him to stand up and stretch out his hand. . . just what the man had been unable to do for years. Jesus is saying, "I'm here today. RISK IT!"

Chapter 5: The woman reached out from a thronging mob to touch the hem of Jesus garment. "Who cares about the crowd? He's here today. I'll risk it."

Chapter 6: Andrew risked it in front of five thousand hungry people when he solved their problem by finding a little boy with five pieces of bread and two small fish. Sure the people laughed. But they got fed.

Chapter 9: The father of a demon-filled son risked it when he said to Jesus, "I don't know what else to do. Please help my unbelief!"

Chapter 10: Blind Bartimeaus, blind son of a blind

father, risked it in Jericho when he cried out, "Jesus, have mercy on me."

Twenty-five years ago, a Baptist evangelist was delivering a more-than-usual fiery sermon. The people were excited about all the possibilities of eternal life here and now. As he raised his voice, the congregation joined in with hearty Amens and Hallelujahs. In the balcony of the church, the people were standing and cheering, "AMEN!" and "PRAISE THE LORD" to show their affirmation of his proclaimed truth.

Leaning a little too far forward in the front row of the balcony, a young lady teetered on the brink of balance, and then fell forward over the railing. The gentleman standing next to her grabbed on to whatever he could hold. It happened to be the back of her dress . . . which did not prove of sufficient strength to stop her fall. There was a squeal of fright, the rending sound of tearing material . . . and then the awful realization that the girl had disappeared over the edge of the balcony.

So there she was . . . dangling by one hand from the banister, in just her basic underwear, the man next to her holding high her dress for all to see, as if to say, "I did what I could!".

The preacher shouted, "If any man looks at that half-naked young lady, hanging over the edge of the balcony by just one hand, he will be struck blind on the spot!"

One little farmer elbowed his wife in the ribs and muttered "I believe I'm gonna risk one eye."

To be a "risker" presupposes "doing". I was at a funeral the other day and as I looked at the young man in the casket, I was sure that not one person in the hall wanted to change places with him. Oh, he wasn't doing anything bad . . . he just wasn't doing. And doing no wrong is not a noble enough purpose or satisfying enough reason for living people to choose.

In my college days we used to chant:
"We don't smoke and we don't chew,
And we don't go with the girls who do;
We ain't got no girlfriends . . . "

When did so many people become experts at "doing no wrong"? Ask anybody anywhere to name the things the Church is AGAINST. The list will go on and on. Then ask what the Church is FOR. The pause will be uncomfortable, long and probably endless.

Whatever happened to the Good News? You know . . .
the possibility of "Thou art . . . thou shalt be,"
the promise "Follow me, I will make you to become ..."
the potential of "He that doeth the will of my Father
shall enter the Kingdom of Heaven."

There has been enough of what we don't do!! We need to work on our "can-do's." After all, that is the purpose and reason for being here.

Of course there will always be critics when you move to the cutting edge of life. People don't always applaud when you step out where the new begins. You do it anyway . . . because it's right. Everything looks impossible to the people who never try anything.

Don't worry about faultfinders and detractors. View them as seasick travelers on the voyage of life, rearranging the deck chairs on the Titanic, all the while complaining that at dinner last night, the gravy was too salty.

A ministry friend of mine published a safe, little newsletter called THE CAREFUL WALK. Man, if I had a newsletter, I'd want the masthead to read OVERBOARD!. You know, get out there with Jesus and take a walk on the water.

Are you aware that when a mother eagle senses it is time to teach her babies to fly, she takes one of the brood on her back and soars toward the sun. Then she TIPS OVER. As the eaglet falls toward the earth, the mother circles it all the way down. Just before it hits the ground, the mother swoops under and carries it high to the sky again and repeats the lesson over and over again.

Finally she brings the baby back to the nest and deposits it safely home. Can you imagine what that first eaglet says to his brothers and sisters? STAY OFF MOMMY'S BACK TODAY!

But without the risk . . . there is no flying . . . and the eagle would forever be left to live with the turkeys.

Mark Twain reminded us about the careful cat who having sat down on a hot stove-lid, learns to never sit down on a hot stove-lid again . . . and that is well. But sadly, she will never sit down on a cold one anymore either.

Only take out of an experience the wisdom that was in it. When you have learned that . . . go ahead . . . dare.

A friend wrote this for me the other day. Let me share it with you. I think it's close to perfect. Try it on for size.

RISK IT

To laugh is to risk appearing the fool.

To weep is to risk appearing sentimental.

To reach out to another is to risk involvement.

To express feeling is to risk exposing your true self.

To place your ideas and your dreams before the crowd
is to risk their loss.

To love is to risk not being loved in return
to live is to risk dying
to hope is to risk despair
to try is to risk failure

But risks must be taken.

The greatest hazard in life is to risk nothing.

The person who risks nothing,
does nothing,
has nothing,
is nothing.

He may avoid suffering and sorrow,
but he simply cannot learn,
feel,
change,
grow,
love,
or live.

Only the person who risks is free!

23

WHEN THEY COULD NOT

George was nine years old and lived next door to a cemetery. Rodney was his best friend, and his house was on the other side of the graveyard. Whenever he played with Rod, George's Dad always came over to walk him safely home. There was something terrifying about that trip back to the house . . . the ghost stories shared by his older brothers, the eerie tomb-stones with their dimmed epitaphs, the shadows that seemed so real and threatening. No matter what was the reason, George was afraid to walk it alone.

But on this particular Friday, unexpected company had come to George's house and Dad just couldn't get away. "You'll have to come home by yourself tonight," Dad said with his reassuring telephone voice.

"But I can't," a frightened George argued. "I'm afraid."

"You have to," Dad stated firmly. I'll be waiting on our front porch and the light will be on. Just keep telling yourself, 'I can do it' and start running. Don't stop until you get here!"

Georgie screwed up his courage, took a deep breath and started running through the cemetery muttering, "I can do it! I can do it! I can do it!"

Unknown to George, the local grave-diggers had been in

the cemetery late that afternoon preparing a site for an early Saturday funeral. So chugging along in the twilight, chanting courageously, "I can do it! I can do it!" George quite unsuspecting fell right into the hole.

Also unknown to George was the fact that the town drunk had been wandering through the field looking for a place to sleep, and had fallen into the same grave. Feeling secure, he had snuggled into a dark corner for the night. You can imagine his surprise when a stumbling nine year old tumbled into his domicile.

He watched silently as George swallowed hard to calm his heart, and whispered, "I can do it!" jumping up on the wall of the grave, trying to climb out. But to no avail. His fingers failed to hold and he slid back to the bottom.

George sighed deeply to stop the tears . . . backed up to one end of the grave . . . took a running start and slammed into the other end and started climbing. "I can do it! I can do it! I can do it!" He was almost shouting as his fingers reached the grass at the top of the ditch . . . but then they lost their grip and slipped. Down he tumbled in a forlorn heap.

"I can't do it," he muttered. "I just can't do it."

The drunk spoke from the shadows, "Sure you can."

. . . And he did!!!

Now that's called MOTIVATION.

Take a look in the Book . . . Mark, Chapter 2, provides an encouraging look at doing what you can't.

There was a huge crowd that day in Capernaum. Jesus was teaching and people were everywhere. Jammed in the home, looking in the windows, trampling down the flowers. We're talking about a serious flock of folks.

Why were they there? Two things to notice:

"Jesus was in the house." (vs. 1) There has always been something fascinating and magnetic about His presence. And it's still true. Where ever He is . . . people will be.

"And He preached the word to them." (vs. 2) To a world full of question marks He offered truth full of exclamation points! And that hasn't changed either. What does God have to say? Find that out . . . and people will rally to hear.

But now comes the drama of COMPLICATION. Four men are bringing a sick friend to see Jesus, knowing that only He can help him. But the mob is so massed, they can't get near the house . . . let alone in the door.

What do you do when nothing works out like you think it should. You do as these four friends did . . . you find a way. A true man is like tea, his real strength appearing when he gets in hot water.

For a long time it seemed to me that whenever real life was about to begin, there was always some obstacle in the way. Something had to be gotten through first, some unfinished business; terms still to be satisfied, a debt to be paid. Then my life would begin. At last it dawned on me that these obstacles were my life!

And you know it. You've failed many times. What do you mean you don't remember?

You fell down the first time you tried to walk.

You almost drowned the first time you tried to swim.

Did you hit the ball the first time you swung the bat?

Don't worry about failures. Worry about the chances you miss when you don't even try.

Now . . . check their COMMITMENT. You have to love it instantly: "When they could not . . . they did it anyway!" (vs. 4). They scrambled up on the roof, somehow carrying their friend, tore apart the thatching and lowered him into the presence of the Master.

Get this: "When Jesus saw their faith" (vs. 5). Now that's an amazing announcement! Most of us have been taught that faith is esoteric and quixotic. It's internalized . . . more like a feeling than a fact. But here it is registered that faith is visible.

It's exactly the point that Jesus' brother James was making a few years later when he declared, "I will show you my faith by my works . . . faith without works is dead."

And we really ought to give some credence to the unsung hero of the miracle. One other person who demonstrated belief by action. It wasn't just the needy man or the four friends. Another hero, unnamed but not unnoticed. It's the man who owned the house with the new hole in the roof.

No protestation from him about the value of private property. (Blessed is the ministry that messes up not the buildings.)

No calling for help to get the loonies out of his ceiling. (Do we have to be so ardent about reaching everybody?)

No searching for agreements to prohibit this kind of activity. (Surely there's something in the by-laws somewhere.)

Don't you love the positive, outreaching attitude of concern? "Whatever it takes to get this man to Jesus . . . do it. I can get another ceiling . . . he may never get another chance."

So there they all are in the home . . . and Jesus does the expected. He forgives the sick man of his sins and sends him on his way with new expectation for life, "Take up thy bed and walk."

You can be sure that this forgiven, healed man had no trouble getting out the door. The same crowd that had blocked the entry into the house now gladly moved aside. It had to be like Moses walking through the Red Sea as the mob divided to make way.

And it is fascinating that everyone, including the skeptics, had one COMMENT in common. "We never saw it like this before." (vs. 12).

The Bible does not need defending today. It needs demonstrating. Showing the world what they have never seen before.

Alice Patterson was a brand new believer and as such, she needed some form of outlet for her service. Fortunately her Church provided plenty of opportunities. But with no background or experience in spiritual matters she felt as out of place as a ham sandwich in a Jewish deli.

Looking over the possible service tasks, she found nothing fitting her potential. Slowly she crossed positions off the list.

Not smart enough to teach Sunday School.

Not talented enough to sing in the choir.

Not experienced enough to play in the orchestra.

Not tough enough to direct park cars in the parking lot.

Not knowledgeable enough to be a guest receptionist.

Then she saw it . . . SUNDAY SCHOOL VISITATION. Alice thought, "Surely, even I can do that."

She showed up on Tuesday night to learn exactly what her responsibilities would be. Sitting with the other volunteers, she was surprised to sense the hurry, scurry and worry of the challenge. The man in charge seemed fussy and distracted. "We are falling far behind with our prospect lists. Tonight, everyone needs to take five cards and complete all the visits before 9. Come back here and we'll make an accurate accounting so we can know exactly where we are for next week."

After a short prayer, he dismissed the visitors with another admonition to haste. Alice took her stack of cards and stopped by the leader for some further information and encouragement. "Can't I take something with me to leave at the homes? Otherwise, I'm kind of at a loss for words."

He shoved an UPPER ROOM in her hands. "This has the Church address and Service Schedules imprinted on the back. You can leave these . . . and please hurry."

Alice got to her first contact-house and nervously rang the bell. A small five-year-old opened the door, but proved unwilling to answer any questions. It was cold outside, so Alice stepped into the plain little home. As the tot ran off to get Mommy, Alice was concerned about his bare feet in the chilly weather.

Mother appeared carrying a baby and followed by two other small children . . . both barefooted. She quietly explained that Daddy was resting. He'd been sick and unemployed for six months. She apologized for the messy house and shoeless children. She had been working two jobs and there just didn't seem to be enough time or money for everything they needed.

Alice fingered her UPPER ROOM and then asked the five year-old to come near. She placed the open booklet on the floor and then traced the tiny footprint on the page. She turned two leaves over and did the same for the other children.

Excusing herself, she hurried to the Eastdale Mall, went into a store and asked a salesperson if he could fit shoes to foot-tracings? The clerk confessed he had never tried that before, but it did sound intriguing. Cutting out the patterns and stuffing them into little shoes took some time, but Alice felt warm and accomplished as she headed back to her first contact-house with the packages.

She barely made it back to Church by 9, the appointed hour for reconvening. She listened to all the reports and nervously waited for her turn. While everyone else was waving wads of accomplishments, she looked down at her one completed card and felt foolish.

And then her name was called. Time for report. Alice was wishing she could say that God had answered her prayers . . . that she had prayed no one would be home . . . and they weren't.

But that's not what had happened . . . so on with the truth. "I don't think I did very well," she began. "I only got to one house."

"One house!" the leader interrupted. "One house! Didn't you get a picture of the energy of the evening. You should have handled all five of yours. Some of these people (he gestured proudly) even came back for more. What in heaven's name happened to you?"

"Well, by the time I got the feet traced and the shoes bought and delivered, my time was up," Alice began.

"Feet traced . . . shoes bought. We don't have time to hear the whole story now. But please do tell us, what did they say when you invited them to Sunday School?"

"I never asked," she confessed.

"You didn't even ask?" was the incredulous leader response. "You didn't ask?"

"I never had a chance. There wasn't time. Before I could say anything, the five-year-old asked me, 'Can we come to your Sunday School someday?'"

And you know they did . . . and kept on coming. Today the whole family is part of the fellowship. I asked them, "What made the difference in your lives? Why Church now?"

Guess what the Daddy told me. Without knowing it, he quoted from Mark, Chapter 2:

"We never saw it like this before."

24

EASY DOESN'T DO IT

Easy doesn't do it! Never has! Still doesn't! Never will! In these days of the "take-it-easy", "good-enough-to-get-by" and "easy-does-it" philosophies, we all need to be reminded that somethings are important enough to give our best to . . . all the time.

The early church in Rome grew rapidly. Eighteen months after Paul's visit, there were 250,000 believers.

The catacombs, underground living places, stretched 19 miles across and were 7 stories deep. They had no platforms, no PA systems, no carpet . . . only an altar.

Those early believers had great grace, faith, love and power.

Some of those who were captured were beaten until they were bloody and then driven out of the city to die.

Others were thrown to the lions in the frenzied "Games" at the colossal Coliseum. They were so full of great grace, faith, love and power that nothing could deter their commitment. They prayed, sang and testified with such fervency that the heathen would jump down from the stands to die with them.

During one martyrdom, a Christian was asked, "What can your Christ do for you now?"

"Three things," came the answer.

"He can cause me to love you.
He can give joy so I can't feel pain.
He can take me home."

Tertillian was a leader in the early Church. He spoke vehemently against giving into Roman power and pressure. One of his targets was the practice of burning incense at the altars outside the work places. Christians were expected to drop in their tribute just like all the tradesmen.

"You can't do that," Tertillian protested. "You belong to Christ."

"But we have to work," someone disagreed.

"No, you don't," Tertillian answered.

"Well, we have to eat," another declared.

"No, you don't," Tertillian repeated.

"But we have to live!" one more added.

"No, you don't!" was Tertillian's response. "You only have to be faithful!"

Nothing "easy-does-it" about that.

The lives of two Romans, one a powerful emperor and the other a lowly citizen, have spoken eloquently to us for twenty centuries.

Both had tremendous power . . . the emperor, power over men; the subject, power with God.

The emperor basked in luxury all his life. The subject was often hungry, and several times he was whipped by civil authorities. Mobs stoned him for his unpopular preaching.

Both visited the Grecian city of Corinth within the space of a few years. When the emperor came, new coins were made in his honor called "advent coins." An inscription was stenciled in stone to immortalize a speech the monarch made during the visit. That inscription, now excavated and deciphered by archaeologists, assumed divine honors for the pompous ruler.

No royal carpet was laid out for the obscure Roman citizen. He obtained employment as a tentmaker. His Sabbaths were spent preaching a new message in the Corinthian synagogue. When he was made unwelcome, he moved to an adjoining house, where for over 18 months he told the Corinthians about a crucified and resurrected man who he declared was the Son of God. Many believed and became followers of this Jesus. And before the itinerant preacher left, the believers were organized into an assembly.

The emperor's speech has long been ignored . . . except by a few historians.

The preacher, on the other hand, wrote two letters to the "saints" at Corinth, one of which contains the greatest treatise on love ever penned, and is still widely used today.

The obedient subject was eventually executed by this blood-thirsty emperor.

Two thousand years later, both men are clearly remembered and easily identified . . . the emperor for his senseless brutality, and the subject for his sacrificial devotion to God.

It was in 64 A.D. that the city of Rome had largely been destroyed by fire. The Emperor Nero was blaming the Christians, and in the mass arrests that followed, Paul was recaptured and returned to Rome.

Imagine this legend with me. Nero tells Paul his punishment for preaching the resurrected Christ is prison . . . the loss of his freedom.

Paul says, "You cannot take my liberty from me. Christ has set me free."

"Then we'll take all your money and possessions. You are a pauper."

"You can't do that," Paul replies. "My treasure is laid up in heaven, where moth and rust don't corrupt, and thieves can't break in and steal."

"Then . . . we'll exile you away from family and friends. Paul, from now on, you're alone."

"You can't do that! I have a friend who sticks closer than a brother."

"Paul, I'll kill you! You're a dead man!"

"You can't do that, either. For me to live is Christ, to die is gain."

Nero shouts, "Get him out of here! I never want to see him again!"

Nero didn't . . . and he never will!

As the soldiers lead Paul away, it really appears that Nero has won this day. He is still gloating on his throne, and Paul is on his way to execution.

But the final score wasn't tabulated there. Here we are today, two thousand years later, still naming our sons Paul, and calling our dogs Nero.

Easy doesn't do it! Never has! Still doesn't! Never will! So let me say this for me and mine . . .

I am a part of the fellowship of the unashamed
  the dye has been cast
    I have stepped over the line
      the decision has been made.

        I won't look back
          let up
          slow down
          back away
          or be still.
My past is redeemed
  my present makes sense
  my future is secure.

I'm finished and done with low living
                  sight walking
                  small planning
                smooth knees
             colorless dreams
            tamed visions
           mundane talking
        cheap giving
        and dwarfed goals.

I no longer need pre-eminence
           prosperity
           position
           plaudits
           or popularity.

I don't have to be right
                    first
                    tops
                    recognized
                    praised
                    regarded
                    or rewarded.

I now live by faith
              lean on His presence
              walk in patience
              lift by prayer
                    and labor by power.

My face is set
  my gait is fast
  my goal is heaven
  my road is narrow
  my way is rough
  my companions are few
  my guide is reliable
and my mission is clear.

I cannot be bought
              compromised
              detoured
              lured away
              turned back
              deluded
              or delayed.

I will not flinch in the face of sacrifice
      hesitate in the presence of adversity
        negotiate at the table of the enemy
          ponder at the pool of popularity
            or meander in the maze of mediocrity.

I won't give up
      shut up
        or let up until I have stayed up
              stored up
              prayed up
              paid up
        and spoken up for the cause of Christ.

I must go until He comes
      give until I drop
      witness until all know
      and work until He stops me.

        And when He comes for his own
        He will have no problem recognizing me . . .
      because my banner will be clear
        my scars will be evident
          my hope will be realized
      and my joy will be full.

      It will be worth it all.

I am a committed believer
      a dedicated disciple
      and a satisfied servant
      of the Lord Jesus Christ!

Easy doesn't Do It! Never has! Still doesn't! Never will!

25

WINNING IS AN
INSIDE JOB

"**D**o you know the secret of success?"
"No, what is it?"
"I can't tell you."
"Why?"
"It's a secret."

That's basically the feeling of people who stand outside looking in. But you know that that's not true. Success is a simple combination of motivation, ability and opportunity. It's taking the challenge, doing the best you can with what you have every chance you get. Someone who knows has suggested that success is 10% inspiration and 90% perspiration. And you can be sure of this . . . the only successful substitute for work is a miracle.

How about education? Can you succeed in life without an authoritative collegiate training? That's an oft asked question . . . and not everyone agrees on one answer. But in truth, formal education has never validated success, nor does the lack of it guarantee failure. Being a winner is always something that springs from within . . . whatever else we get is added. Imagination is more important than knowledge, because knowing offers no assurance of doing. Yes, you can reach the top in business and in life, regardless of your external opportunities and educational achievements . . . and, from some experts who missed college, here are 10 ways to do it.

1. WORK "CAN'T SEE" HOURS. Start work when it's so dark you can't see and finish when you can't see because it's dark again.

Bill Rosenburg,
Dunkin' Donuts founder

2. LOVE WHAT YOU DO . . . AND DO IT! Don't procrastinate. And don't think. Do it. Thinking is the enemy of creativity. You can't think about things. You simply must DO them.

Ray Bradbury
Science Fiction author

3. GIVE THE CUSTOMER VALUE FOR THE MONEY. Putting a good product at a reasonable price in front of a customer likely means he'll come back. And if he does, your business is a success.

Harold Butler
Founder of Denny's

4. START SMALL. Set short-term goals. Great dreams are often so far away from your reach that you can become discouraged. But each small goal you achieve gives you confidence to try the next.

John H. Johnson
Publisher of Ebony

5. BELIEVE THAT NOTHING IS IMPOSSIBLE. It doesn't matter how many times you fail in trying to get something to work. All you need is one success.

Jack Goeken
Founder of MCI Telephone Network

6. TRY TO LEARN FROM OTHER PEOPLE. Then once you get a good grasp of what is going on, say what's on your mind and do what you think is right. Your goal should always be to be the very best at what you do.

Jay Darling
President of Burger King

7. FIND A NEED AND FILL IT. But never resort to gimmicks! If you fill a real need, you'll have a loyal following.

Adrien Arpel
Cosmetic Queen

8. KEEP YOUR WORD. If you say you'll do something, do it. What is needed . . . and wanted . . . in the world are people who will do what they say they'll do. And think really big. If you have the courage to stand up and say, "This is what I want to do," and do it, you can be successful.

William Millard
Founder of ComputerLand

9. LEARN FROM YOUR MISTAKES. Too many people, when they make a mistake, just keep stubbornly plowing ahead and end up repeating the same mistakes. I believe in the motto, "Try and try again." But the way I read it, it says, "Try, then stop and think. Then try again."

William Dean Singleton
Co-owner of MediaNews Group Inc.

10. SET YOUR PRIORITIES. Seek ye first the kingdom of God and His righteousness, and all these [good] things shall be added unto you.

Jesus Christ
Owner of the Universe

Don't you love the unexpected? You know . . . the "hook" in a story, the punch line in a joke, the solution to a "whodunit". And I especially enjoy it when the just-plain-good-guy wins . . . and the antagonists have to swallow hard. Here's my latest favorite:

A newly appointed preacher by the name of Gooch wrote his first report to the Conference. It stunned the District Superintendent because it was obvious the new man was an abject illiterate and had been pawned off on him by another District Superintendent. Here is what the freshly assigned pastor wrote:

> I'm sennin you the report you axed fer. I ain't been on this here nu pointment but six muns and the report ain't so gud. I ain't had but leven to jine the chuch on that perfeshun of faith, but I got me six Baptists and two Piscolopeans. We dun paint the chuch inside an out, and bot them perty new red songbuks you tole us about. We tuk all them portionments you giv us and we dun paid them out too. I am working on a butter report nex time. We gonna have us some reneul in this here chuch.

Before the illiterate preacher could be called on the carpet by the District Superintendent for his sloppy language, this note came from the brother:

We dun paid over and above that worl survice and them
bennevolunes and we aim to get a passel more money for
thim missum specials. I got me one of thim long black
things to preach in. I ain't figured out if I shud
take my coat off fore I put it on or leave it on under.
It's purty, but it shore is hot. But I reckon it helps
my surmens, cause we tuk in 8 more members in the last
cuple weeks."

At that, fearful if he did call the brother on the carpet, and
fearful if he did not, the District Superintendent dumped the
problem in the lap of the Bishop. In the next edition of the
conference paper, the brethren were amazed to see both
letters printed . . . and this notation from the Bishop:

"We ben spendin two much time tryin to spel instead of
tryin to sel. Let's keep an i on the missum of the
chuch. I want all the brethren shud reed these letters
from Gooch, who is doin a grate job for the chuch, and
you shud jest otta go out and do like he dun."

John Wooden, UCLA basketball coach extraordinare said,
"Never let what you cannot do interfere with what you can
do." Find a opening . . . a piece of opportunity . . . and stick
to it. Today's mighty oak is merely yesterday's little nut that
managed to hold its ground.

God is always looking for people who are willing to be
used. Availability, adaptability and responsibility are His
priorities in the search for servants. What great thing you can
do for God has never impressed Him. What is offered to Him
gets His attention . . . every time.

The Master was searching for a vessel to use.
Before Him were many. Which one would He choose?
   "Take me," cried the gold one, "I'm shiny and bright.
   I am of great value, and I do things just right.
   My beauty and luster will outshine the rest
   And for someone like You, Master, gold is the best."

The Master passed on with no word at all
And looked at a silver urn, narrow and tall.
   "I'll serve you dear Master, I'll pour out your wine.
   I'll be on your table, whenever you dine.
   My lines are so graceful, my carvings so true
   And my silver will certainly compliment you."

Unheeding, the Master passed on to the vessel of brass
Wide mouthed and shallow and polished like glass.
   "Here, here," cried the vessel, "I know I will do.
   Place me on your table for all men to view . . ."

The Master came next to the vessel of wood
Polished and carved, it solidly stood.
   "You may use me, dear Master," the wooden bowl said,
   But I'd rather you used me for fruit, not for bread."

Then the Master looked down on a vessel of clay,
Empty and broken it helplessly lay.
No hope had the vessel that the Master might choose
To cleanse and make whole, to fill and to use.
   "Oh, this is the vessel I've been hoping to find.
   I'll mend it and use it and make it all mine.

I need not the vessel with pride of itself.
Nor one that is narrow, to sit on the shelf.
Nor one that is big-mouthed and shallow and loud.
Nor one that displays its contents so proud."

Then gently He lifted the vessel of clay,
Mended and cleansed it and filled it that day.
He spoke to it kindly,
   "There's work you must do.
   Just pour out to others what I pour into you."

26

PLEASE . . . NO PEAS!

It was in Junior High that I met the stoic master of mathematic mayhem, Miss Williams, dispenser of algebraic knowledge. KEEP SMILING was posted on every wall of her classroom. One might as well have hung KEEP COOL signs in the raging inferno of Hell. Nice sentiment . . . but hardly practical to the situation.

Being persuaded that my college career hinged on my success in Miss Williams class, I sought desperately to please her. Even stayed after class to impress her sometimes. (Didn't work. I still had to turn in assignments.)

One super-puzzling problem kept me in her presence one April afternoon. All my friends were long gone . . . enjoying the freedoms of after-school life. But I was determined to get that answer.

Finally I moaned, "I wish I knew the answer," hoping for some academic pity.

"The answer is easy," she assured me. "I have the answer book right here in my desk drawer."

"Well, the answer's not easy for me," I protested. "Why don't you just get the book out and tell me. Then we'll both get to go home."

"Oh, no," she insisted, "It's working through the equation that teaches the lesson."

Four pages of calculations later, I was done. The answer? Zero! "All that work for NOTHING," I muttered.

"No . . . not for nothing," she rebutted. "You just learned the difference between answers and solutions."

I never forgot Miss Williams . . . or her lesson. She taught me something valuable about the processes of God. The perplexities of life are to be worked out . . . not zipped through like magic. Getting to the answer is often more important than finding what the answer is.

One of our problems is that we expect Jesus to appear in a celestial helicopter and snatch us out of the marsh and mire of each swampy dilemma. But that's not the plan. If you're lost in a quagmire of life, you need to climb a high tree, and locate a distant fixed point . . . a mountain, another exceptionally tall tree, or a bright light . . . anything that remains immovable and unchanging. You move that direction for as long as you can . . . then when you feel confused again . . . you climb up for another glimpse of the distant perspective.

He provides us with perspective . . . so, using His instruction and direction, we can find our way out of the circumstance.

Understand this . . . the Bible never does say that Jesus is the answer. It only says that Jesus is the way.

Night was falling in the forest and the hunter was absolutely confused. His guide was staying in the grove and handed the tenderfoot a burning torch and saying, "If you hurry, you can get back to camp for the night."

"But I don't know the way," the man protested.

"Just follow the path and the tree markings. It's the same way we came," insisted the escort.

Studying the closing darkness, the man worried aloud, "Do you think the light on the torch will last the whole way?"

"It will if you start now," came the stoic reply.

Never be guilty of waiting for a rescue. Start looking for light . . . and get going. "In everything give thanks." That's what the Bible says. I'm really glad it doesn't say, "In everything feel grateful!" The two are very different, you know. Feeling grateful is easy when things go just right. But they don't always do that. I mean sometimes God seems just as interested in afflicting the comfortable as He is in comforting the afflicted. That's because He wants to build character more than He wants to make people feel good. And the bumps of problems produce a finer quality of character (like the bite of frost makes sweet apples) than the ease of comfort (no rain makes a desert).

When problems come (and be sure they will) you have three options: Resign, Resent or Rejoice. The choice is yours!

1. RESENT THE STRUGGLE. Pitch a fit, pout a lot, and pull out your martyr card so folks can punch it for you. Throw a pity party. Be sure to tell yourself that no one understands you. Nobody can judge an Indian until he has walked in his moccasins.

Then figure that what is wrong for others is all right for you because you are different.

If you do not believe this, turn the coin over and say, "Well, if I am wrong, at least I have plenty of company.

Then, too, you should convince yourself that no one loves you and they will be sorry some day for their indifference.

Keep telling yourself that you have as much right to happiness as anyone else and write the ticket your own way. After all, if you don't take good care of your own self, who will?

By all means, feel sorry for yourself and be thoroughly convinced that you are the only one in the world who has suffered the things you have.

When, because of this, people begin to avoid you, tell yourself it is their fault and that as Christians they should be more considerate.

Find someone else you can find fault with. This way you won't have to face reality with yourself.

When the sky falls and life grows meaningless, simply ask yourself how God can be so mean?

2. RESIGN YOURSELF TO THE TRIAL. Shrug your shoulders and mutter, "Oh, well, nothing's gonna turn out all right anyway." Surrender yourself in morbid, fatalistic fashion. Become a moper and groaner. It's easy to go around sad of countenance and make the world the more gloomy because of your presence in it.

> Count your worries, name them one by one;
> Think that vict'ry never will be won.
> Face your problems, count them o'er and o'er;
> All your disappointments and vexations sore.
>
> When you are discouraged, feeling all is lost,
> Say the prize you're seeking is not worth the cost;
> Think about your troubles, name them o'er and o'er,
> Every time you count them, there will be one more.

If you see a promise fits you to a "T",
Though you hunger for it, cry, "It ain't for me."
Say you cannot help it, you are made that way,
God is not your refuge, nor your strength or stay.

You must bear your burdens, sink beneath the load,
Find your way to heaven is a dreary road;
Tho' He solemnly declares, "I'll give you rest,"
Worry over everything, for that is best.

WHY PRAY WHEN YOU CAN WORRY?

3. REJOICE IN THE TEST. So you have problems!! Who doesn't? Trials and difficulties are the common denominator of life. Whenever your cup of joy is full . . . there is always somebody around to jostle your elbow.

So what are you going to do? Give up and throw away the container? Try to figure out what went wrong while you clean up the mess? Or get right to the task of refilling the cup?

I vote for the last.

However tough life may be . . . it's better than the alternative. Life is not a cafeteria line where you can just pick out what you want. It is a full course meal . . . and you get it all from soup and salad to gravy and dessert. So you might as well decide to make the best of it.

One morning shortly after Christmas I woke early, studied the ceiling for awhile and dreamily shared with my wife that for the first time in months I had nothing to do. No project clamoring for completion, no music to write for tomorrow, no squeaky wheels to oil. I could just relax . . . "Soul, take thine ease."

Not more than ten minutes later the phone rang with an

administrative problem that would add a new dimension to the word disaster. It put both my feet on the floor and sweat on my brow.

I got one of those wonderful wifely smiles and the accompanying words of wisdom, "Looks like God thought of something."

He knows it's not good for me to have time when I'm coasting. I need constant pressure to keep me leaning on the Rock. When heavy storms come they push you to your knees . . . and what's wrong with that.

So ask me how I'm doing. GREAT!! God noticed me today.

By the time she was 18 months old, Julie could spot a serving of peas across a crowded table. The reaction was always the same . . . eyes closed, tongue out and her little body shuddering with chilly anticipation. Someone had shared with me that all children needed green vegetables to round out their diet. Peas were as green as I knew and my first born was not about to be deprived of what was necessarily hers.

So they were smothered in butter, buried in mashed potatoes and covered with chocolate syrup (no attempt to ingest the greenery was overlooked). But no matter what . . . the butter disappeared, the potatoes were gone and the syrup dissolved. And out of the mouth rolled little green balls . . . usually unscathed. The only thing peas seemed to accomplish was getting other things green . . . napkins, bibs and Julie's complexion, whenever I managed to sneak some inside her.

I relaxed my campaign for green vegetables when I noticed that every meal was rated in Julie's mind by peas. When she was 4 she went next door for her first "dinner away", and when she returned, I asked what her friend's mother had served.

"Peas," came the quick response.

"But what else?" I persisted.

Her eyes flashed and she said it strongly, "She gave us peas."

"No mashed potatoes, or Jello salad with bananas, or roast beef or ice cream?" I asked knowingly.

Her lower lip came out and I saw the beginning of a tear form in her eye as she turned toward the bedroom. "Peas," she muttered one more time.

Even when she knew she didn't have to eat them, she'd keep one eye suspiciously in their direction as if they'd sneak up by themselves and hide on her plate. A whole Thanksgiving Dinner could be ruined by a bowl of peas at the other end of the table.

I know so many Julies . . . focusing so much on what they don't like, they never notice all the good things spread on the table of life.

Let me give you the good advice that saved Julie's enjoyment: FORGET THE PEAS!!

And remember, "He carrots for you." But that's another story.

27

GOING THROUGH
THE MOTIONS

Last December there was an accident, a terrible accident, at the National Zoo in Washington D.C. The caretakers were in shock. It seems the ants that live in a glass-fronted display case in the Invertebrate House got excited. "They got too ambitious and worked themselves up," said Ed Smith, the man who cares for the leaf-cutting ants from Trinidad.

What the ants did, quite by mistake, was remove the head of their queen. The workers were trying to transfer their egg-laying monarch from the chamber where she has resided for the past four years since being shipped from the Cincinnati Zoo. Apparently the hole they were trying to pull her through was small . . . and the queen wasn't. Pop!

Ant specialists refuse to speculate on whether an ant can feel totally stupid. Basically, scientists think of ants as amazing little machines, driven by their genes, which act in concert with a world that they know largely through smell.

That is why an interesting thing is now happening at the Invertebrate House. The workers are still tending their dead queen. They are continuing to hold her in the same position. As long as she still smells like the queen, they will care for her.

So there her body hangs on display, the headless thorax and abdomen suspended from the ceiling of her royal chamber, her back to the roof, legs dangling loosely. Or rather the two legs she has left. The other four mysteriously disappeared the same day her head did.

Well . . . where is the head? Did the workers eat it? "No," Smith observed, "I don't think so."

Is it on the trash heap outside the nest, where the ants deposit their dead and discard pieces of their fungus garden?

"No, the head is someplace in the nest," Smith said. "But wherever it is, you can be sure they're taking good care of it."

That means that somewhere nestled among the legs and loving mandibles of her attendants, the ants are bringing food and trying to feed that dead head. (A guess about what they are doing with the legs would only be reckless speculation.)

Meanwhile, back in the royal chamber, the queen's body rests. (It also would be reckless speculation to infer that she misses her head.)

Anyway, among insects, heads are overrated as body parts. Indeed, the queen could continue to lay eggs for hours or even days after her head was removed. "She seems to be doing pretty good headless," Smith observed. "Heads aren't as important as you might think."

Still, removing the queen's head from her body was not a good plan, Smith admits. Sooner or later, probably in weeks, the queen's head and body will stop smelling like the queen and start smelling dead. The bacteria will start their work. Even royalty rots.

The colony, eventually, is a goner. A queen from this common tropical species can live as long as 14 years. But without a queen, there can be no eggs. That is all a queen does. She is a virtual egg-laying machine. No eggs . . . no workers.

The eggs and larvae that are now being tended will be reared by the workers, but eventually the colony will age and finally wind down.

At present, all seems strangely normal in the colony. Life goes on. The ants are in what our psychologists would call the denial stage. The bigger workers are still collecting the leaves that Smith puts out for them and carrying chiseled bits of greenery back to the nest, where smaller ants masticate the bits and place them in their gardens, while still smaller workers plant thin hairs of fungi, which produce spores that feed the wormlike larvae and workers.

But alas, Smith reports that the colony's brood contains no winged ants, which are the sexual ants, the virgin queens and males. Every ant in the nest now is a sterile female worker, with the exception of the headless queen, so there is no chance of the colony saving itself.

Imagine those ants . . . making believe the queen is still alive . . . going through the motions . . . feeding a dead head that must be singing, "I Ain't Got No Body." There are a lot of people like that! Big pretenders.

You know . . . the lumberjack whose axehead breaks off the handle. Immediately, he is confronted with two options. Stop and get a new head . . . or keep on swinging the handle real fast so no one will notice it's gone.

Or the television addict whose cable has been disconnected but still sits in front of the TV and tells you everything's OK if you don't mind looking at snow.

How about Samson . . . the mighty man of scripture? He compromised his way down from lofty conquests for God to the lowly couch of a Philistine harlot. Originally empowered by the Spirit of God, he was shocked, shackled, and enslaved when he rose up as before to slay the enemy and was powerless because of his spiritual concessions.

And these are the saddest words in Scripture: "He wist not that the Lord was departed from him." Samson's power was dissipated . . . and he didn't even know it. Going through the motions of flexing his muscles, staring disdainfully and snarling menacingly just didn't work any more. Samson had become a great pretender.

And you remember Saul? Now there was a giant of a man in every way. He towered head and shoulders above everyone else and had a heart to match his size. And courage! From the start he was a King who moved and acted decisively, with deeply spiritual motivations. Scripture records that "God gave him another heart . . ." and "the Spirit of God came upon him . . ." He was a divinely appointed and God-powered leader.

Saul garnered prestige. But that began to affect his relationship with God. No one noticed anything for a while, but Saul and God were not enjoying the mutually cordial relationship they had in the beginning. Saul began to think he was all-important and that he had all the answers. It was an irritation to Saul when God insisted on being the CEO.

Some new tactics were in order. First, Saul tried to *bribe* God through a lot of fancy and expensive gestures designed to buy His favor. He wanted to obligate and manipulate God by means of elaborate gifts. He wanted to get God under his control. This was Saul's basic flaw. He was, in effect, putting himself ahead of God. As my good preacher-friend, John Ed Mathison says, "If God cannot be President . . . He will not be resident."

When Saul discovered that God could not be bought, owned, or used, he tried another approach . . . he wanted to be a *buddy* with God. Count on this . . . it is always the man who is really far from God who thinks he can use this approach to the Almighty. The farther a man is from God, the more self-righteous and self-satisfied a man becomes.

Saul spoke magnanimously of God as his private protector. In fact, he presumed that his personal plans were always God's plans. Gradually he becomes the man whose conscience is always clear. He is correct in everything he does and a simple explanation suffices as justification for all his actions. Saul grows to think that he can do no wrong.

God, however, has no special buddies. God is God. Even Saul begins to get the point eventually. So his next move was to *be* God. But he quickly discovers that he cannot quite organize the entire universe the way he would like. It is not as easy to be God as he had thought. So Saul is driven to his knees in prayer. But it is the wrong kind of prayer . . . this is the prayer of a man who is trying to *bully* God. His words have the tone of a threat. He says in effect, "You do this . . . or else, Lord . . ."

You know that no man ever forces God's hand. He will not be intimidated. Saul's final act in his relationship with God is to try to *bury* Him. He turns to the flimflam of spiritualism and contacts, he thinks, the dead prophet, Samuel. All of this to be a statement that God no longer existed for Saul. Saul had buried God! The divine has been disposed of. Saul is on his own. So listen to these words, "The Spirit of the Lord departed from Saul." That which had made him great was gone. And he never knew it. Another great pretender.

After murdering God, Saul continued on a relentless path of terror and intrigue. He tried to kill the young David, threw a spear at his own son, Jonathan, had a family of priests at Nob massacred . . . eighty men, women, and children slaughtered in cold blood! He became a man at war with the whole human race. He was against everybody and believed that everyone was against him.

The final murder Saul committed was self-murder. He took his own life at the battle on Mount Gilboa when everything was going against him. Actually Saul had been committing suicide for years by putting himself in God's place and assuming the role of Master of Life.

You know, there are two Sauls in the Bible . . . the King we just discussed . . . and an apostle who changed his name from Saul to Paul. Both died violent deaths . . . one at his own hand, the other at the hand of a vicious Emperor. Their epitaphs were strangely similar . . . five words each . . . and three of those words identical. Listen:

SAUL . . . I HAVE PLAYED THE FOOL

PAUL . . . I HAVE KEPT THE FAITH

Never let yourself just go through the motions. Don't be guilty of playing games or laying grass at the dead head of a mocked majesty. Always be sure that what you are doing is really necessary and counting for something bigger than you are.

I will forever remember the story related to me by Butch

Barkman, now in charge of JAARS, the aviation wing of Wycliffe Bible Translators. When he returned from piloting a flight in Peru, two Missionary Administrators stepped out of his small plane at the end of an arduous jaunt, one rather smirkingly said to the other, "Do you realize that in the last four days, we have traveled more miles than the Apostle Paul did in all his missionary journeys combined?"

A mechanic, standing at the other end of the jungle hanger, never looked up from his work as he asked, "Yes . . . but did you accomplish as much?"

28

FAITH IS CONTAGIOUS

Parenthood! What a shame to waste it on people so young. Let's face it . . . when you start having babies, you're not sure of what's going on. None of us start out with any experience, which, of course, is what you get just after you've needed it.

We all know that faith is not hereditary. There is nothing spiritually automatic about "like father, like son." Kittens may be born in an oven, but that doesn't make them biscuits!

In one sense faith is a very private and personal thing. It is a consummation of choices and commitments made by an individual.

But on the other hand, did you know that faith can be passed on from parent to child? Oh yes it can . . . it's in the Book! With Mother's Day just past and Father's Day nearly here, my heart has been thinking a lot about parents and children and faith.

You remember the story in Mark 9 about the concerned Father and his speechless son, and the Ruler of the Synagogue who feared his daughter was dead (Matthew 9) and the Mother who besought Jesus (Mark 7) for her demoniac daughter? Well, through the faith of those parents something of faith happened to their children.

Paul writes to Timothy and says, "I call to remembrance the unfeigned faith that is in thee, which dwelt first in thy grandmother Lois, and thy mother Eunice, and now in thee also."

Hear it again . . . faith is not hereditary. But it is contagious!!

Faith's reward . . . is faith stronger in you,
　　　　　　　　　　brighter in others,
　　　　　　　　　　focused in Him.

Parental wisdom is bringing up your children so that someone else will like them besides you.

Children are natural mimics. They act like their parents in spite of every attempt to teach them good manners.

If a child lives with criticism, he learns to condemn.
If a child lives with hostility, he learns to fight.
If a child lives with ridicule, he learns to be shy.
If a child lives with shame, he learns to feel guilty.
If a child lives with tolerance, he learns to be patient.
If a child lives with praise, he learns appreciation.
If a child lives with fairness, he learns to show equality.
If a child lives with security, he learns to have faith.
If a child lives with acceptance, he learns to find love.

We all know what we want our children to get from us. Probably, most of us have made lists from time to time, underlining these salient verities. But did you ever wonder what a list from your progeny might look like? Try this one on for size . . .

A MANIFESTO FROM YOUR CHILD

1. **Don't spoil me.**
   I know quite well I ought not to have all I ask for.
   I'm only testing you.

2. **Don't be afraid to be firm with me.**
   I prefer it.
   It makes me feel more secure.

3. **Don't let me form bad habits.**
   I have to rely on you to sense them in the early stages.

4. **Don't make me feel smaller than I am.**
   It only makes me behave stupidly "big".

5. **Don't correct me in front of people if you can help it.**
   I'll take much more notice if you talk to me privately.

6. **Don't make me feel that my mistakes are sins.**
   It upsets my sense of values.

7. **Don't be too upset when I say, "I hate you."**
   It isn't you I hate.
   It's your power to thwart me.

8. **Don't protect me from consequences.**
   I need to learn the painful way sometimes.

9. **Don't take too much notice of my small ailments.**
   Sometimes they get me the attention I need.

10. **Don't nag.**
    If you do, I shall protect myself by appearing deaf.

11. **Don't make rash promises.**
    Remember that I feel let down when promises are broken.

12. **Don't forget I cannot explain myself as well as I would like.**
    I'm not always as articulate as you.

13. **Don't tax my honesty too much.**
    I am easily frightened into telling lies.

14. **Don't be inconsistent.**
    That confuses me and makes me lose faith in you.

15. **Don't put me off when I ask questions.**
    If you do, you will find that I stop asking and seek my information elsewhere.

16. **Don't tell me my fears are silly.**
    They may be to you but they are terribly real to me, and you can do much to reassure me if you try to understand.

17. **Don't ever suggest that you are perfect or infallible.**
    It gives me too great a shock to discover you are neither.

18. **Don't ever think that it is beneath your dignity or position to apologize to me.**
    An honest apology makes me feel very warm toward you.

19. **Don't forget that I love experimenting.**
    I couldn't get along without it, so please put up with it.

20. **Don't forget how quickly I am growing up.**
    It must be very difficult for you to keep pace with me. But please try.

21. **Don't forget that to thrive I need lots of understanding love.**
    But I guess I don't need to tell you that, do I?

They really don't have to go any farther, do they? That list gets me to my knees . . . every time. A few years back when Re'Generation was still on the road, we included this in our presentation for one year. See if it helps you . . .

A PARENT'S PRAYER

O Heavenly Father, make me a better parent. Teach me to understand my children, to listen patiently to what they have to say, and to answer all their questions kindly.

Keep me from interrupting them or criticizing them. Make me as courteous to them as I would have them be to me.

Forbid that I should ever laugh at their mistakes or resort to shame or ridicule when they displease me.

May I never punish them for my own selfish satisfaction or to show my power.

Let me not tempt my child to lie or steal but guide me hour by hour that I might demonstrate in everything that I say or do that honesty produces happiness.

May I ever be mindful that my children are children and that I should not expect of them the judgment of adults.

Let me not rob them of the opportunity to wait on themselves and to make decisions.

Bless me with the bigness to grant them their reasonable requests and the courage to deny them the privileges I know could do them harm.

Make me fair, just and kind, and fit me, O Lord, to be loved, respected and imitated by my children, and help me always remember that better parents raise better children.

People who wonder where the younger generation is headed for would do well to consider where it came from.

I took a piece of brand-new clay
And idly fashioned it one day;
And as my fingers pressed it still,
It bent and yielded to my will.

    I came again when days were past;
    The bit of clay was hard at last.
    The form I gave it, still it bore,
    But I could change that form no more.

        I took a piece of living clay
        And gently formed it day by day,
        And molded it with power and art . . .
        A young child's soft and tender heart.

        I came again when years were gone;
        It was a man I looked upon.
        But early imprint still he bore,
        But I could change him then no more.

Usually parents who are lucky
in the kind of children they have,
have children who are lucky
in the kind of parents they have.

29

A FARTHER FATHER

It was their son's first visit home from college and he was met at the front door by his parents. First thing they noticed was how strangely he was dressed. Unmatched colors, baggy clothes, and an overall unkempt appearance.

Dad said, "It's really nice to have you home, son ... but you really look like a fool!"

Grandpa came down the stairs, laughed and said, "You look just like your father did when he came home from college."

The son replied, "Yeah, that's what he just told me!!"

Listen to these two boys talking.
"Hey, Bobby!"
"Yeah?"
"Do you believe in a real live devil?"
"Nah!"
"Really? How come?"
"Well, I think it's like Santa Claus. He's your father!"

Sometimes, I guess, we Dads do come across in strange ways. Like the Little League coach who was talking to his team saying, "In this league we don't lose our tempers, we don't swear and we are not bad losers. Do you understand?"

The team nodded in unison.

The coach continued, "Can you handle that?"

Again the boys unanimously agreed.

"Good," sighed the coach. "Now . . . do you think you can get that across to your fathers?"

It gets confusing. When you're a kid, they don't understand you. When you become a Dad, the kids don't understand you. Sometimes you don't even understand you! But hang in there. It's just a little longer until our offspring will be right in the same spot we are . . . covered with diapers, cereal, kisses and confusion.

The other day I heard one father say about his two sons, "I taught them everything they know . . . and they're still idiots."

But sometimes it's the kids who feel that the grown-ups are the boneheads. Another friend moaned through his perplexity, "I don't know . . . I've got TV, cable, two phone lines, a cellular phone in my car and a fax machine. And my girls still tell me I'm out of touch."

And still one more added, "Kids . . . either a pain in the neck . . . or a lump in the throat."

But age usually brings wisdom . . . if not tolerance . . . and we all grow to appreciate the exuberance of youth as well as the sagacity of maturity.

So who changes? We all do! Wasn't it Mark Twain who said, "When I was 18 my Father seemed the perfect fool? And then when I was 21, I couldn't believe how intelligent he had become in just 3 years."

To further the thought, let me pass this on to you out of my Father's Day files from years past:

WHEN I WAS . . .

4 years old: My Daddy can do anything.
7 years old: My Dad knows a lot, a whole lot.
8 years old: My Father doesn't quite know everything.
12 years old: Oh well, naturally Father doesn't know it all.
14 years old: Father? Hopelessly old-fashioned.
21 years old: Oh, that man is out of date. What did you expect?
25 years old: He knows a little bit about it, but not much.
30 years old: It's amazing how wise he got in the last few years.
35 years old: We need to find out what Dad thinks about it.
50 years old: What would Dad have thought about it.
60 years old: My Dad knew everything.
65 years old: I wish I could talk it over with Dad one more time.

A father is a thing that is forced to endure childbirth without an anesthetic.

A father is someone who gets very upset when the first report cards aren't what he thought they should be. He scolds his son . . . but he knows it's the teachers fault.

Fathers grow old faster than other people . . . that's because mothers can cry where it shows. Fathers must be strong outside and die inside.

Fathers have very stout hearts. So they have to be broken sometimes or no one would know what's inside.

Fathers are what give daughters away to other men who aren't nearly good enough so they can have grandchildren smarter than anybody's.

It's easier for a father to have a child than it is for a child to have a father.

You might expect this . . . but the greatest Father I ever knew was mine. The perfect blend of discipline and warmth,
compassion and constraint,
faith and reason
hope and reality
strength and flexibility
demonstrator and demander
teacher and player,
example and explainer.

He was a white collar man in a blue collar world . . . Superintendent of Warehouses for a large furniture chain in the San Francisco Bay area. So good at being a boss that he was voted the best in the country three years in a row . . . by the men who worked for him.

For a class I was teaching to infanticipating partners, I made a list. Here it is for you . . . just as they got it. All caps . . . no comments. These truths speak for themselves.

LESSONS FROM MY DAD

1. A MAN'S MAIN JOB IS TO TAKE CARE OF THE PEOPLE WHO DEPEND ON HIM.

2. NEVER BOAST, NEVER PRETEND, NEVER SAY ANYTHING THAT ISN'T TRUE.

3. SHARE WITH THE LESS FORTUNATE.

4. WHEN YOU SAY YOU'RE GOING TO DO SOME THING, DO IT.

5. WHEN YOU'RE RIGHT, DON'T QUIT.

6. DON'T TURN YOUR BACK ON FRIENDS WHO ARE DOWN AND OUT.

7. IT DOES NO GOOD TO COMPLAIN.

8. THE ONLY REASON FOR BEING LATE IS NOT STARTING SOON ENOUGH.

9. TALK WITH YOUR CHILDREN.

10. WHEN THE GRASS IS GREENER ON THE OTHER SIDE OF THE FENCE, IT'S TIME TO FERTILIZE YOUR LAWN.

11. WHEN YOU SEE A TURTLE ON A FENCE POST, YOU KNOW HE DIDN'T GET THERE BY HIM-SELF.

What a man! What a study! What a heritage! That's being a Farther Father. Going beyond the limits. Painting outside the lines. Giving a glimpse of everything good and possible. Everybody ought to have a father like that! And guys, if you didn't have one . . . then be one!!

Like this one. Every time the young man said to his father, "Pop, can I have $10?" he'd give him 5. Once he said, "Pop, I need 500 bucks." Next day, on his bureau was $500.

So he asked, "Pop, I don't get it. I say give me 10, you give me 5. I say 500 . . . and the whole thing is on my dresser. Why?"

Dad replied, "Listen, if you need 10 or 5, that's for nonsense. If you need 500, you must be in trouble, and that's what a father is for."

And that's being a Farther Father.

Charles Adams was an Ambassador during the administration of Abraham Lincoln. As you might imagine . . . his life was full of challenging schedules. Pressures and demands were heavy on every hand.

Persuaded by his wife, he took his one son out for a day of fishing. Ambassador Adams secretly chaffed under this fatherly obligation. There were just too many pressing things to do to be caught up sitting in a boat watching a line bob in murky water.

To make things worse . . . they caught nothing. Absolutely nothing! He wrote in his Journal,
"Went fishing and caught nothing.
We spent the time drowning worms.
A totally wasted day."

But his son's version of the trip was totally different:
"Went fishing with my Dad.
Greatest day of my life!

You know how kids spell love?   T-I-M-E.

Maybe the most moving moment of my fatherhood came one day when my second grade daughter handed me a note.

Slowly scrawled in careful penmanship, with the letters going up hill and getting smaller on their journey. But I had neither time nor inclination to adjudicate the offering. My eyes stung at the thought, my heart was overwhelmed by the message and my mind reeled at the responsibility:

I'M WAITING TO GROW UP JUST LIKE YOU.

30

YOU'RE JUST LIKE GLUE!

It is, without a doubt, the most creative job in the world.
It involves taste,
    fashion,
       decorating,
         recreation,
           education,
             transportation,
           psychology,
            romance,
             cuisine,
               designing,
                 literature,
                  medicine
                    handicraft,
                  art,
                      horticulture,
                    economics,
                    geriatrics,
                      entertainment,
                        maintenance,

purchasing,
  direct mail,
    law,
      accounting,
      religion,
        energy
          and management.

Anybody who handles all that has to be somebody special.
She is.
She's a mother.

Let's start with this:

You can fool all of the people some of the time,
and some of the people all of the time,
but you can never fool MOM!

"Hey, Mom, you're just like glue!" At first she didn't understand. She was just returning from the hospital and it had seemed like such a long time. But now she was home again, and he was beside himself with excitement. As soon as he could put his thoughts together and into words, Sonny exclaimed, "Mom, you're just like glue! "I mean . . . you hold us together. When you're gone, we fall apart. Sally lives in one place, Buddy somewhere else, and Daddy and I have to get along by ourselves. You're the stuff that keeps us stuck . . . just like glue!"

A mother is what makes you put on a sweater when she feels cold.

A mother makes you eat spinach 'cause it'll give you good,

strong teeth. (She ought to feed it to Grandpa!)

Mothers like the bony pieces of chicken, the burnt pieces of toast, and the smallest pieces of cake.

They like to hoe the longest row and carry the heaviest load.

They know all about things like sugar cookies, band-aids, puppies, Christmas wishes, and broken hearts.

They fix toys that will not run and noses that will not stop.

Mothers write on the hearts of their children things the world will never erase.

The wise mother lets the father wear the pants in the family. She just provides the suspenders.

It's a mother's privilege to have children, her right to love them and her duty to let them go. Have them, love them, let them go. The last, they say, is the hardest of all.

What an influence Mothers are . . . by behavior and belief. Some Mothers have never figured that out . . . but if they only knew what they were logging into the psyche of their youngsters. How about these Mothers for fogging the issue . . .

MRS. WRIGHT: Orville and Wilbur, you'll never get that bicycle shop off the ground.

MRS. FULTON: Robert, what's got you all steamed up.

MRS. FRANKLIN: Ben, go fly a kite.

MRS MORSE: Sam, stop tapping your fingers on the table . . . you're driving me crazy!

MRS. LINDGBERGH: Charles, can't you do anything by
yourself?

MRS. WASHINGTON: George never did have a head for
money.

MRS. ARMSTRONG: Neil has no more business taking
flying lessons than the man in the
moon!

So Moms . . . be sure your belief behaves. We need all the
help and support we can get. Did you know that in the Greek
language, the feminine form of LORD is LADY. And there
is good reason for that . . . for the most part, Mother applies
the principles of home and influences greatly the destiny of
the children.

A wise man said, "Children are volumes of blank paper,
and upon them will be written the record of Mother's life."
The modern challenge to twentieth century motherhood is
as old as motherhood itself. It is the eternal challenge . . . that
of being godly women. That very phrase sounds strange in our
ears. We never hear it now. We hear about every other kind
of women . . . beautiful women,
smart women,
sophisticated women,
career women,
talented women,
single women . . .
but so seldom do we hear of a godly
woman.

Susannah Wesley had 19 children, including John and Charles, the founders of the Methodist Church. The following is the set of rules she strictly enforced. It's an insight into why those children turned out so well.
1. Allow no eating between meals.
2. Put all children in bed by 8:00.
3. Require them to take medicine without complaining.
4. Subdue self-will in a child
5. Teach each one to pray as soon as he can speak.
6. Require all to be still during family worship.
7. Give them nothing that they cry for, and only that which they ask for politely.
8. To prevent lying, punish no fault which is first confessed and repented of.
9. Never let a sinful act go unpunished.
10. Never punish a child twice for a single offense.
11. Commend and reward good behavior.
12. Any attempt to please, even if poorly performed, should be commended.
13. Preserve property rights, even in the smallest matters.
14. Strictly observe all promises.
15. Require no child to work before he can read well.
16. Teach children to fear the rod.

Suppose, just for Mom, there were a version of the Love Chapter, I Corinthians 13. Well . . . there is now . . .

If I speak words of discipline and rebuke to my children, or even words of Scripture, but have not love, I am only a nagging voice of a persistent annoyance.

If I have the gift of housekeeping and can make all beds

and wash all clothes, and if I have a faith that can move children to pick up toys, but have not love, I am nothing.

If I give all to the Salvation Army and surrender my savings to the mission field, but have not love, I gain nothing.

Love forgoes sleep to rock a child; love gives a million drinks of water cheerfully.

It does not cringe when friends show up in the latest fashions, or with tickets to Hawaii.

It does not presume to excel in mothering skills.

It is not boastful of its own children's accomplishments.

It is not impolite when son or daughter refuse to obey.

It is not begrudging when its own plans are sidestepped in lieu of a scraped knee or lonely moment.

It does not throw objects or abusive words and does not slam doors when opposed.

It keeps no record of unappreciated limousine service, unmade beds or under the table crumbs.

Love does not delight when somebody else's child is screaming at the grocery store, but rejoices to offer a look of sympathy.

It always preserves its own family's honor, always expects

growth and progress, always looks beyond the spilled milk and honey-sticky hair, always continues despite the discouragements.

Love never fails.

But whether there be household chores, they will cease; whether there be temper tantrums, they will be stilled; whether there be dirty diapers, they will pass away.

For we understand our children only in part, but then we will see their hidden fears and dreams.

When I was a child, I threw temper tantrums, I left my room a mess, I rebelled in disobedience.

When I became a mother, I hid those childish ways behind me so no one will ever see them.

Now we see chocolate-smeared cheeks and sleep-tousled hair; then we shall see the hidden potential of a creative and valuable child.

Now I know dirty clothes, cobwebs and a busy schedule; then I will see the Lord Almighty, angels and redeemed loved ones.

And now these three remain: cooking, cleaning and love; but the greatest of these is love.

I was twelve when I took my catechism classes in the Pastor's Study. One Saturday afternoon he explained to us what it meant to be a Christian, and then asked if any of us had ever thought of modeling our lives after anyone we knew.

One by one we responded. Some had never thought of any one person as a ideal Christian. Others had been impressed by the life of some Sunday School teacher, Church Leader or Preacher.

My turn finally came. I was very shy at that age so I had waited till last. Not because I didn't have an answer . . . but because I thought no one would care. When the Pastor asked again if I knew some Christian whose life I thought worthy of imitation, I answered, "Yes. I'd like to be like my Mom."

He said he understood why.

31

NOT FOR SALE

Let's talk about cost. Every commodity of earth has its worth. One article of merchandise exceeds another in value. The relative cost of real estate may vary. The rate of stock may differ on the exchange. Yet all these properties are bought and sold on the market, and to each is affixed a price.

Much of the territory now included in the United States once bore a price tag. There was the Louisiana Purchase, and Seward's Folly (otherwise known as Alaska) which found their way into our history book by way of the check book. California, Nevada and Utah were purchased from Spain. We bought much of our nation from the Indians, including Manhattan Island. And all this for a price!

Today, we even compute war in dollars and cents.

We have become accustomed to evaluating almost everything with which we are acquainted on a strictly monetary basis. Whether it be an education, a lakeside cabin, a trip abroad or a new bass boat, we make the dollar sign the pivot point. All else is made to revolve around it.

We all know that happiness can't be measured by one's wealth. For instance, a man with $8,000,000 may not be a bit happier than a man with $7,000,000.

Money is what things run into and people run out of. Money no longer talks . . . it just goes without saying.

Of course, money isn't everything, according to the people who have it. But we all know that if your outgo exceeds your income, your upkeep will become your downfall.

We just got a new television set at our house that is three dimensional. It gives us height, width and debt.

It used to be that a man who saved money was a miser. Nowadays he's a wonder. Think about it . . . today people find themselves living in more expensive houses . . . and they haven't even moved!

Did you know it costs about $125.00 a mile to push a cart through the grocery store.

There are bigger things than money. For instance, bills. Money isn't everything. For one thing, it isn't plentiful. But then money can't buy love, health, happiness . . . or even what it did last year.

Money may buy the husk of things, but not the kernel. It brings you food but not appetite,
> medicine but not health,
> acquaintances but not friends,
> servants but not faithfulness,
> days of joy but not peace of mind.

But who can estimate the value of a soul? Who can fix its price? Jesus asked in Mark 8:36-37, "What shall it profit a man, if he shall gain the whole world, and lose his own soul? Or what shall a man give in exchange for his soul?

Did you ever stop to compute what it cost those people in Biblical times to turn away from God? What was in their minds? They didn't get a fair return on their investment.

ESAU .... one bowl of porridge		$ .75
GOMER .... a homer and a half of barley		$13.00
THE UNJUST DEBTOR. . .imprisoning a friend		$20.00
JUDAS .... 30 pieces of silver		$ 17.50

Neither will you! The soul is not for sale. All earth's vast stores of wealth and treasure are not enough to buy a soul. Place on the counter the cities with their skyscrapers, hotels and factories, and the sum would be inadequate.

Add the six continents with all their precious minerals and resources, and still the amount would be insufficient. The earth with its mountains, plains and seas, its gold, silver and oil, its diamond and pearls . . . even the staggering wealth of these could not purchase one immortal soul!

Made in the image of God, the soul is ageless. When the ancient hills and seas have found their graves, and the stars have dwindled like dying candles and been smothered in darkness, the soul will still be young. Created with perpetual youth and endless life, it shall abide the enduring eons of the everlasting ages.

Let's talk about cost. I have heard with astonishment, the voices of people who say they can't accept Jesus Christ because it would cost them too much. Cost them too much! They have no I idea of value or importance. Cost them too much? My response to that has always been, "If I didn't know Jesus Christ as my personal Saviour, it would cost ME too much!" Look at what I'd have to give up . . ."

The only lasting joy I ever found,
  A real purpose for being alive,
    A fountain of real satisfaction;
      A friend who really cares about me,

Someone who cared enough to take my place,
Someone who loved me enough to die for my sins.

In my problems, He's my counsellor.
In my ignorance, He's my teacher.
In my journeys, He's my guide.
In my disappointments, He's my joy.
In my distress, He's my helper.
In my storms, He's my rock.
In my burdens, He's my friend.
In my trouble, He's my comfort.

When I'm weak, He's my strength.
When I'm worried, He's my calm.
When I'm poor, He is my wealth.
When I'm lonely, He's by my side.
When no one else understands, He does.
When everyone else would turn me away,
He says,"Come unto me."

Turn my back on the One who changed my existence?

Leave the One who has come to mean more to me than life itself?

There's is no way that I could ever give up this great salvation!

I could never afford not to be a Christian.

It would cost too much.

Let's talk about cost. He was young, he was loved and he was blind. From the rich farm lands of Nebraska, he had been sent to the Mayo Clinic to see if anything could be done to restore his sight. The neighbors donated the transportation and the local Rotary Club took care of the living expenses. All the family could do was endure the anxiety and wait for the results.

When the bandages were removed, there was good news ... Bobby could see. And there was bad news . . . not nearly enough money to pay the bills. Dr. George Ralph, Senior Opthalmolgic Surgeon, decided to donate his services to this happy youngster, and spoke with the hospital officials about doing the same.

Finally, the healing process was over and Bobby was ready to go home. He gratefully stopped by George Ralph's office. After the final hugs, tears and thanks, little Bobby held out his most precious possession . . . a much used Teddy Bear. While Bobby had been blind, he had lavished his love on the little bear by feeling and squeezing, so now the ears were frayed, the nose was crooked and one of the button eyes was long lost.

The Doctor took the Teddy just to feel it . . . but Bobby said, "I want you to have it. Maybe it will help pay for me."

Today, if you visit the office of Dr. George Ralph, you will find under a glass bell on one corner of his desk, Bobby's Teddy Bear, with this card of explanation,

**THE HIGHEST FEE EVER COLLECTED
FOR PROFESSIONAL SERVICES.**

Let's talk about cost. What was the ultimate price paid for your souls liberation? Heaven stooped down to this world in mercy. Earth, hide yourself in shame among the constellations! Stars of heaven, blush as you run to put on mourning! Little man, throw yourself in shame into the dust from which you came! He whose eyes first reflected the glitter of a sun and watched the fiery trail of the comet through boundless space has looked at a cross. He whose hands once formed the stars and fashioned the pattern of the nebulae felt the nails. He who existed before time and place, and at whose feet someday every knee shall bow, has been crowned with thorns, shed His blood and died for the sins of the world.

And God could not watch. Too great the pain . . . too much the suffering . . . too heavy the grief. Many a Mother felt some of God's agony when she received a telegram from the War Department stating her boy had been killed in action. Through her agony, one mother cried, "I never knew giving a son could be so expensive!"

> If you only had one son,
>> would you send him to this earth
>>> to live in lowly birth
>>>> where no one felt his worth?
>>> God did!

> If you only had one son,
>> would you let him leave his throne
>>> and come to live unknown
>>>> and face his task alone?
>>> God did!

> If you only had one son,
>> would you let him serve and bless
>>> a crowd that offered less
>>>> than love and faithfulness?
>>> God did!

> If you only had one son,
>> would you let him weep and grieve
>>> for men who won't perceive,
>>>> but only make believe?
>>> God did!

If you only had one son,
 would you let him pay sin's debt
  for men who soon forget
   and live without regret?
  God did!

If you only had one son,
 would you let him bleed and die
  upon a cross held high
   between the earth and sky?
  God did!

If you only had one son,
 would you raise him from the tomb
  to lift away the gloom
   from earth with still no room?
  God did!

If you only had one son,
 would you send him back again
  to face a world of men
   who still are lost in sin?
   God will!
   God will!!
   GOD WILL!!!

32

WHO SAYS YOU
DON'T COUNT?

Once upon a time ... in the big little state of Rhode Island ... they were electing a state legislature.

There was a thrifty Federalist farmer who started for the polls late in the afternoon and, on the way, heard the squealing of a pig. He looked around to see the pig with its head caught in the mesh of an old wire fence.

Hogs often will kill and eat a trapped pig. So the farmer stopped to rescue the porker and was too late at the polls.

Now, wait a minute. The Federalist farmer was too late to vote ... and ... the election was decided by a one-vote margin in favor of the Democrats.

If the farmer had been at the voting place in time, the Democrat would not have been elected.

At the following session of the legislature (those were the days when the legislatures elected our Senators) a Democrat was sent to the Senate from Rhode Island by a one-vote margin in the legislature.

Try to keep up with this. The legislator was elected by one vote and his one vote elected a Senator.

And in the United States Senate the vote that we should go

to war with England was carried by the one Democrat margin. So the Revolutionary War was fought because . . . a Rhode Island pig got caught in a fence.

Dr. George Benson of Harding College traced this sequence: One morning in 1844 a grain miller in De Kalb County, Indiana, was walking toward his mill. It was election day, but he had work to do and did not intend to vote. Before he reached the mill, however, he was stopped by friends who persuaded him to go to the polls.

As it happened the candidate for whom he voted won a seat in the state legislature . . . by a margin of one vote.

When the Indiana Legislature convened, the man elected from De Kalb cast the deciding vote that sent Edward Allen Hannegan to the United States Senate.

Then, in the United States Senate the question of statehood for Texas came up . . . the result was a tie vote.

But Senator Hannegan, presiding as President pro tempore, cast the deciding vote from the chair.

So Texas was admitted to the Union because a miller in De Kalb County, Indiana, went ten minutes out of his way to cast his one vote . . . just one vote.

You want more? Thomas Jefferson was elected President by one vote in the Electoral College. So was John Quincy Adams. And so was Rutherford B. Hayes . . . elected President . . . by one vote.

One vote gave statehood to California, Idaho, Oregon, Texas, and Washington. All those people in all those states are United States of Americans because of somebody's one vote.

Kentucky came into the Union as a slave state . . . by the casting of one majority vote in the Constitutional Convention. Had it not been for the one vote, Kentucky would have entered the Union a free state. If it had, Missouri, largely settled by Kentuckians, would have done likewise. In that event there probably never would have been a war between the states.

And closer to home . . . the Draft Act of World War II ... passed in the House of Representatives . . . by just one vote.

So you see, it is important that your voice be heard. No matter how important, or unimportant, you may think it is. Martin Niemoeller, a German Lutheran pastor who was arrested by the Gestapo and sent to the concentration camp in Dachau in 1938, wrote these words:

"In Germany, the Nazis first came for the communists, and I didn't speak up because I wasn't a Jew. Then they came for the trade unionists, and I didn't speak up because I wasn't a trade unionist. Then they came for the Catholics, and I didn't speak up because I was a Protestant, Then they came for me, and by that time there was no one left to speak for anyone."

Martin Niemoeller was freed by Allied forces in 1945.

It was during the Korean conflict that Scott Peterson was mortally wounded. A home-town friend crawled to the side of his dying buddy and asked, "Anything I can do for you?"
With his last breath Scott replied, "Two letters. Write two letters for me. One to my mother. Tell her I died a believer

and I'll meet her in heaven. Write the other to my Sunday School teacher, Mrs. Gunderson. I want her to know I never forgot what she taught me."

The two letters were posted immediately. Mom's reply was slow in coming. It was understandably hard for a loving mother to acknowledge the death of her only son in writing. Mrs. Gunderson's surprising answer came by return mail: "God forgive me. I quit teaching Sunday School eleven years ago. I thought it was all in vain."

Everything counts. We all bear fruit. Nothing is worthless.

Abraham Lincoln referred to that in his Gettysburg Address, "The world will little note nor long remember what we say here, but it can never forget what they did here."

Emerson put it this way: "What you are stands over you... and thunders so that I cannot hear what you say to the contrary."

Five year old Amy was busily working on her art project. Droplets of paint were splattering everywhere as a result of her frenzied activity. "I wanted to get this finished before the last bell," she explained.

"Well, what is it?" queried the teacher.

"Oh, it's a picture of God," Amy stated scarcely pausing in her work.

"But no one knows what God looks like," said the smiling instructor.

Amy looked up and proudly said, "They will when I get through!!"

While home was still in California, my oldest daughter was in Jr. High. I noticed one day in the San Diego Evening

Tribune that twenty-four students had been arrested at her school for possession of narcotics. Jr. Highers! I couldn't believe it!!

The next day I checked the paper before supper . . . and it had happened again! This time seventeen 7th and 8th graders. At the dinner table I casually asked Julie if she knew any of these kids.

"Oh, sure. They're all my best friends!"

Not words of great comfort to a father. I suggested that we spend a little time in conversation after dessert was done . . . and she readily agreed. It never was hard for Julie to talk. We sat down in the den and I assured her that she didn't have to say anything at all. No confessions . . . no denials. I just wanted to share some things from my concerned fathers' heart.

She nodded O.K., so I continued . . . talking about my feelings on the subject and how I was absolutely sure that she could lose her mind, her life, even her soul if she ever got involved.

I paused . . . and she asked if I had finished. I said yes and she said, "Can I say something?"

"Of course . . . if you want to."

"I just wanted to know why you thought I'd do anything like that?"

"Well," I hedged, playing for some time . . . "I guess I'm just a nervous Father . . . and everybody's doing it."

She looked me right in the eye and said, "Diddy . . ." She's always called me Diddy. Still does. "Diddy . . . I'm not everybody!"

What a great line! I'm not everybody. I went to my office the next day and wrote a song for my Jr. High Choir to sing. Don't worry . . . I'm not going to try to sell you some music now

... but you do need to hear the words of the chorus:

> I'm not everybody,
> Everybody's not me;
> God made me a somebody,
> And that's what I'm gonna be.

It was only 5:30 in the morning, so it seemed a little unusual to see a teenage boy walking on the beach. Most of his friends were just getting to bed after some late hour parties, and here he was starting the day.

An old gentleman watched as the young man bent over time and again, picking some object off the sandy beach, and tossing it into the ocean.

After some time the elder asked, "What are you doing?"

"Throwing starfish back into the surf," came the reply.

"I can see that for myself," retorted the man. "I asked what are you doing? You know . . . why this ritual?"

"If these starfish are still on the beach when the sun comes up, they'll die. So I'm throwing them back into the ocean. I'm saving their lives."

The old man snorted, "That's the dumbest thing I ever heard of! There are millions of starfish laying up and down this beach. They're all gonna die. What you are doing is absolutely inconsequential!"

The teenager picked up another, looked at it closely and then said, "Not to this one!"

33

IF WE WOULD WIN SOME ...WE MUST BE WINSOME

Jeremiah, our nine-year-old, sat at the dinner table near tears. When Mommy asked him the reason, he blurted out, "Some kids at school say they don't like me . . . and I don't know why!"

We delayed dessert for a family conference. Stephanie wasn't too thrilled at that prospect, but her grief was assuaged with the promise of a bigger helping at a more appropriate time. (Big sisters are seldom interested in little brother's social problems. In fact, when her Sunday School class was asked, "Which of the Ten Commandments can be applied to family relationships?" she was the one who replied, "Thou shalt not kill!")

We all decided at the family filibuster that Jeremiah could only work in one direction. It would be easy to sit around and: (A) Discuss how unfair some people can be. (When some people say they'll meet you half way, they think they're standing on the dividing line.)

(B) And how foolish these people are to be missing Jeremiah's friendship. (Stephanie thought that one was pretty funny . . . so we hurried on.)

(C) How silly anyone is to pass judgment on any one else. (You can't throw mud without losing ground.)

No . . . working on the outside, trying to fix up the other people, that's never the answer. Not for Jeremiah . . .
>not for you . . .
>not for anybody.

The secret is always to work on the inside. We have to start with the I in l-I-f-e. You remember the old camp song, Kumbyah? "Come by here, Come by me." You really are all you have to work with.

So we formulated some WINSOME CLUES for Jeremiah. He started with one, conquered it (or at least confronted it) then moved on to #2 (without forgetting #1). He never knew what the next clue would be . . . so anticipation as well as achievement played a role.

Just for fun . . . and inspiration . . . here they are for you.

HOW TO HAVE FRIENDS

Clue #1: SELF CONTROL! Nobody cares for the person who is going off like a half-cocked pistol, ready to shoot at a moment's notice. You know . . . the kind of person who approaches every subject with an open mouth.

Clue #2: LISTEN! God gave you two ears and one mouth. That ought to teach you something. Want to be unpopular? Watch the guy who is . . . his mouth works faster than his brain . . . he says things he hasn't even thought of yet.

Clue #3: DON'T BE THE BOSS! Learn to take orders and play on the team. Lots of people want to be stars and very few want to make up the Milky Way. The guy who is bossy all the time is the kind of person who can stand up and rock the boat and make you believe he is the only one who can save you from the storm. Forget being him.

Clue #4: KNOW WHEN TO STOP! Funny is nice ... but only to a point. It's important to see when people start to look another direction. Teasing is OK ... but only for a little while. We never should try to get laughs at someone else's expense.

Clue #5: THINK AHEAD! Always ask, "How will this affect my friends?" "Am I going to be a leader and good example if I do this?" Popular people are the ones who others want to be like.

Clue #6: DON'T CHANGE THE RULES! Discover what other people expect. Go along with them. If you're playing games (or hard at work) it always is the same ... find out who's in charge and don't change things unless you talk it over first.

Clue #7: BE RESPECTFUL! It is very important that you honor other people's property, time and position. Don't use things that aren't yours. Never borrow. If a person is busy, don't bother him. I had a boss who from time to time placed a plaque on his desk,

IF YOU HAVE NOTHING TO DO
DON'T DO IT HERE

I got his message!

Clue #8: USE GOOD MANNERS! Nobody likes sloppy . . . except maybe some pigs. Unless you're planning to join them, be polite, be courteous, be thoughtful. My Mom used to say, "Manners are just happy ways of doing things."

Clue #9: DON'T TALK GROSS! Watch your mouth. By examining the tongue of a patient physicians find out the diseases of the body, and philosophers the diseases of the mind. Usually the first screw that gets loose in a person's head is the one that controls the tongue.

Clue #10: BE HAPPY! You catch more flies with honey than with vinegar. Being positive attracts people to you and makes them feel good. Nobody is drawn to grumpy, negative people who are always complaining.

Clue #11: ALWAYS SHARE GOOD NEWS! Let somebody else pass out the gossip. Act like you like people . . . all people . . . and they'll like you!

Jeremiah is still working on his list . . . and there are still more clues to add . . . but he's on his way. And we haven't had tears at the dinner table for quite a while now.

And then I thought . . . is it as important that they like me as much as they like Him? You know . . . HIM! And then I asked, will my acquaintences like Him if they don't like me?

So all this is important for all of us if we are to be effective witnesses for the Lord Jesus Christ. There must be some fascinatingly captivating things about our lives and behavior to draw them to Him.

Think about sharing your faith this way: It's not just

obligation and responsibility, but it's opportunity, potential, and possibility.

"Help for today and hope for tomorrow" . . . that's a message anyone is glad to hear. Just be sure you're winsome when you try to win some.

Maybe this will help . . . it is not our responsibility that every person comes to Christ. But it is our responsibility that Christ comes to every person.

I love the way Reggie White, Defensive End of the Philadelphia Eagles puts it: "I'm nobody telling everybody about somebody who can save anybody!"

Two ministerial students from Samford University in Birmingham, Alabama, decided they would spend some of their summer doing evangelistic work in a rural area near Montgomery. One hot day they stopped their car in front of a farmhouse and proceeded up the path through a gauntlet of screaming children and barking dogs.

When they knocked on the screen door, the woman of the house stopped her scrubbing over a tub and washboard, brushed hair and perspiration from her brow and asked them what they wanted.

"We would like to tell you how to obtain eternal life," one of the collegians answered.

The tired homemaker hesitated for a moment and then replied, "Thank you, but I don't believe I could stand it!"

Obviously you want to be more careful than that about communicating the whole concept before you try to land a convert.

I have a good friend in Alabama who is an outstanding,

competitive bass angler. He's entered plenty of tournaments . . . and won his share.

If you know anything about the Bass Anglers Society, you will remember that they never used to announce the location for the contest until the week of competition. That was to prevent anyone from taking an unfair advantage by fishing the waters before the other competitors could get a try.

But some of the tournaments went a bit sour when no one seemed to be able to figure out which lures and enticements the local bass would appreciate the most. After one tourney, when very few bass were landed . . . the participating sponsors complained. They could only sell equipment on the basis of success. Find a way to catch bass in greater quantity.

More fish . . . more sales! So it was that the Bass Anglers determined to announce the venue six months prior to competition.

Remember my friend . . . Gary? Building contractor in Montgomery . . . and the tournament was to be held at Lake Eufalla . . . which is not far south of Alabama's State Capitol.

Gary spent a lot of his early mornings on the Lake . . . not fishing . . . but checking where the fish were and what they responded to. He carefully kept a master chart on light meter readings, water temperature and air temperature.

The day the competition began, he pulled out his chart, gauged the brightness of the daylight along with the air and water temperature, decided the fish were "over there" and would enjoy "this" for breakfast.

Gary not only won the meet, he set a record for pounds of bass caught in a single day as well as tourney total.

Besieged by reporters after his stunning success . . . the most frequently asked question was: "Who did you emulate?"

"I don't understand your question," was Gary's first response.

"Who did you copy?"

"What method did you find most effective?"

"What fisherman's style did you use?"

"Who did you study?"

Gary's thought-provoking answer: "I didn't study the fishermen. I studied the fish!"

What a great line for all of us fishers-of-men. Study the fish . . . and represent the Savior. That's really all there is to it.

Throughout French history, when a young soldier or sailor was missing in action, a memorial service was held in his hometown where a member of the family or a close friend would stand in his place. As the name of the service man was read, the friend would rise and say, "He died for France."

One terribly sad day, a grief stricken Mother in this moment of emotion forgot the line . . . and then forever changed it. As her son's name was called as missing in action, she stood and said, "I am here for him."

34

NEVER SING ALONE

"Help yourself." I heard that over and over again from our considerate hostess the other afternoon. We were enjoying some fellowship and relaxation and I really lost count of how many times she said it. Want a glass of water, a towel, a new ping pong ball? "Help yourself." The answer was always given in gentle love and invitation, but with strong overtones of personal responsibility. Everything you want is readily available and just waiting for you. "Help yourself."

There is really nothing wrong with wanting to be happy, you know. It's the getting there that causes the problem. Actually, it may be that the best way to help yourself . . . is to help someone else. You need to be kind to your friends. If it weren't for them, you'd be a total stranger.

Friendship moves beyond acquaintance into trust and affection and support. Love may be blind, but friendship tries not to notice or pass judgement too quickly.

But a real and lasting friendship passes even deeper than that. The Apostle Paul admonishes us to weep with them that weep and rejoice with them that do rejoice The first part of that is a whole lot easier than the second, because anyone can sympathize with the suffering of another person but only a friend can sympathize with his exploits.

An acquaintance of mine says that the biggest problem with being successful is finding someone who is happy for you.

Friends can give without remembering . . . and take without forgetting. We do good to and for each other . . . and never keep score.

It is never too soon to do a kindness . . . because we never know how soon it will be too late.

Love for one another is still the greatest cure the world has ever known . . . for whatever the problem. Because love works both ways . . . it's not only beneficial to the <u>givee</u>, it also works wonders for the <u>giver</u>. It is one of the most beautiful compensations of life that no man can sincerely help another without helping himself.

Job learned that lesson. You remember how he was tormented and tested by Satan, his so-called friends . . . even his wife. He lost his lands, livestock, family, and finally his physical health.

Job got out of his mess when he applied one very simple truth to his problem. "God delivered Job out of all his trouble when he prayed for . . . "

You guessed what? His health?
His finances?
His personal needs?
His family problems?

None of those!

Get the truth . . . "God delivered Job . . .
out of all his trouble . . .
when he prayed for . . .
HIS . . .
FRIENDS."

Focus on friendship. Important? Let's talk about it!

Lasting friendship lasts, you know . . .
through the years and the tears,
the sad and the glad,
the crown and the down.

A friend is someone who makes you feel totally acceptable.

A friend is someone who asks how you are . . .
and waits for the answer.

A friend is someone who knows all about you . . .
and loves you anyway.

A friend is someone who walks in . . .
when everyone else walks out.

A friend is someone who hears the song in your heart . . .
. . . and sings it to you when your memory fails.

Love is a flower but friendship is a tree.

One of my best friends . . . out of my Collegian Ministry days in San Diego wrote this for me. It needs to be shared with you . . . because it's worth it.

FRIEND!

I bet you keep your pockets full of treasures
that you freely spend
on chasing blues
and changing moods
and bringing sadness
to an end

and spare parts
just for patching dreams
that no one else can mend

And the world too seldom sees that kind of friend!

I bet your smile's the formula for every special
secret blend
of sunshine's trace
some far-off place
and gold that's found
at the rainbow's end

and for every life
without a song
your heart finds one to lend

And I thank you for being that kind of friend!

Gail Romaine

An old animal legend tells of the day that an elephant and a woodthrush were discussing whose voice could be heard at the farthest distance. The elephant insisted his was, while the woodthrush was positive that his voice could be heard across the entire forest. They decided on a test. The elephant confidently arranged to go first. At the sound of his trumpeting voice the earth vibrated and the trees shook. Animals big and small ran for shelter and cowered in fright.

With a triumphant smile the elephant nodded, "Your turn." The woodthrush flew to the highest tree and began to sing a song that was beautiful and true. The notes sailed into the forest and the frightened animals came out of hiding to listen. From tree to tree and bush to bush the song traversed the timberland and came out on the other side as beautiful as it had been at the beginning.

An inspection committee was sent out to check the results of this LOUDEST VOICE CONTEST. "Did you hear the elephant?" was the first query. "Yes, of course. That frightening bellow invariably sends us running in fear," said all the animals near the source of the sound.

"And the bird?"

All the animals nodded yes. "We heard it . . . that sweet song of the woodthrush always brings peace to our hearts. We love that sound."

The questions and answers were the same all through the forest. But at the far end of the weald no one had heard the elephant's voice. "What elephant? We heard no roar. He must have been too far away."

But had they heard the bird? "Oh, yes," everyone agreed. "That lovely, peaceful song. We know it and love it and look forward to it."

The committee came back with their report. The wood-thrush had won. His song was heard much farther than the elephant's roar.

"How can this be?" the elephant wanted to know. "My voice is bigger and louder. It shakes the trees and quakes the ground. How could someone not be aware of me and yet hear the sound of a simple, little bird?"

The woodthrush answered, "It's because when you yell, you yell alone. But when one of us sings, another picks up the song and carries it on . . . from tree to tree and forest to forest. You see, we don't sing just our own song . . . we all sing the song of our brother and sister. . . and you can hear it through the forest, across the plain and around the world . . . because when we sing, we never sing alone.

35

THE SONG THAT IS SEEN

It was Sunday and I was worried about the five-year-old twin girls scheduled to sing for the Evening Service. Usually, it was standard procedure for me to plan, or at least audition, all the special music and/or drama for that weekly (that kept it from being weakly) "Happening".

But this time I was outmaneuvered by a well meaning Grandmother who bypassed the customary and got directly to the Pastor, assuring him that the girls were cute, talented and hers. (Two out of three wasn't bad.) But they could not be there in time for any rehearsal. Not to worry . . . "Trust me," she said.

The girls got to the platform just before the announcements and offering time (seemed the safest time to me) and did look really great. Matching pink dresses and berets, with white lace-topped sox and shiny, black patent-leather shoes.

Grandma handed them off to the Pastor who introduced them, and hand in hand they delivered their well practiced song. But the congregational smiles turned soon to chuckles and then to outright laughter as the meaning of the song broke through.

You got the picture? Adorable five-year-old twins singing with great gusto and scintillating sincerity,

> YEARS I SPENT IN VANITY AND PRIDE,
> CARING NOT MY LORD WAS CRUCIFIED.

Really? Somehow the genuineness of the lyric escaped us all. It's just too hard to believe a child that young could sink that far into sin so soon. Then I began to think . . . what if the songs we so often sing were really done in an candid and straightforward manner. You know . . . if we really sang what we meant . . . it might come out like this:

> When morning gilds the skies,
> My heart awakening cries,
> **OH NO, ANOTHER DAY.**

> Amazing grace how sweet the sound,
> That saved a wretch like . . .
> **YOU.**

> I love to tell the story . . .
> **HAVE YOU HEARD ABOUT JIM AND SALLY?**

> The church's one foundation . . .
> **IS TAX DEDUCTIBLE.**

> I love Thy Church, O God,
> Her walls before me stand;
> **BUT PLEASE EXCUSE MY ABSENCE, LORD,**
> **MY BED FEELS SIMPLY GRAND!**

A charge to keep I have,
A God to glorify;
BUT PLEASE DON'T ASK FOR CASH FROM ME,
THAT PRICE COMES MUCH TOO HIGH.

Am I a soldier of the cross,
A follower of the lamb?
YES! THOUGH I SELDOM PRAY OR PAY,
I STILL INSIST I AM.

Must Jesus bear the cross alone,
And all the world go free?
NO! OTHERS, LORD, SHOULD DO THEIR PART,
BUT PLEASE DON'T COUNT ON ME.

Praise God from whom all blessings flow,
Praise Him, all creatures here below!
OH, LOUD MY HYMNS OF PRAISE I BRING,
BECAUSE IT DOESN'T COST TO SING!

Now ... back to reality and sincerity. That we sing in public worship is Biblical and vital. How we sing is just as important ... maybe more so.

In the sixteenth century Martin Luther freed hymnody from its monastic prison and restored the ancient privilege of congregational singing. The Lutheran Church became a singing body. We read of crowds of people singing chorales in churches, market places and even the streets.

Today we can lift our voices in song with the same enthusiasm, understanding and deep spiritual feeling. The Apostle Paul described the way we should sing hymns when he said,

"Be filled with the Spirit; speaking to yourselves in psalms and hymns and spiritual songs, singing and making melody in your heart to the Lord."

Hymn singing is not an art to please the music critic. It is melody from the heart to please God. The purpose is not to appeal to the feet, to satisfy the popular taste for the sensational or trivial, nor is it for relaxation or entertainment. Hymns give an opportunity for each worshiper to express his deepest inner, spiritual feelings.

The psalmist says, "Let all the people praise thee." This would indicate that a variety of hymns is required to enable everyone to praise God. A limited number may result in such frequent repetition that hymns become mechanical, even threadbare, losing their purpose of aiding in worship. No loyal Christian will firmly lock his lips in a silent revolt against an unfamiliar hymn. Each congregation should earnestly seek to learn new hymns that will give a wide range of spiritual expression and that will meet the varying tastes found in every congregation.

The congregation should follow the leadership of the director, the organ and the choir. Hymns should not drag in tempo, becoming heavy and ponderous instead of inspiring and uplifting. Descants sung occasionally by the choir, with floating obligato soaring heavenward, can heighten the effectiveness of a festive hymn.

To be really right, a spiritual song must come from the heart and go to the heart. Technically, a hymn is directed to God, while a Gospel Song is addressed to people. In either case, it is still true . . . a heart to heart declaration. When that is really happening, it is a song that is seen. Seen in faces at the moment. Seen in lives through the week. Seen in eternity as the effects go on and on and on and on and on and on and on.

That's exactly what the Psalmist David had in mind when he penned, "The Lord hath put a new song in my mouth . . . many shall SEE it and trust the Lord." It's the song that is seen.

You've heard of James Cash? A bright, young, successful salesman from Hamilton, Missouri. So successful that within a year the long hours of hard work broke his health and the doctor told him to go West . . . or die!

James chose West . . . got well and started back to work for a drygoods firm in Wyoming. His ambitious spirit caught the eye of his employers and he moved to Kemmerer to manage a brand new store. Out of his earnings he would be allowed to buy a one-third interest.

James and his bride lived over the store with meager furnishings and bare necessities, and in six years he bought that store and two others . . . for $30,000 cash.

He put his name over the front door . . . JAMES CASH. Oh, he liked the looks of that. He wanted more.

He struggled and failed. Management was not his forte. His health broke again . . . so he moved on . . . got well . . . and started over.

By now James had learned to employ other persons as he had been employed. To allow each store manager to earn a share of the business. To divide its profits or its losses.

James added more links to the chain, more stores to the string until twelve years later he was operating seventy-one stores . . . all with his name over the front door.

Another three years . . . 177 stores.

By 1928 there were more than a thousand stores across

America . . . all with his name, James Cash, right over the entrance.

Then . . . 1929.

With the crash also fell his fortune. He borrowed more and more to keep his empire and philanthropies going.

One day . . . suddenly . . . he was broke. Fifty-six years old and 7 million dollars in debt. Now he really got sick! Penniless, James Cash, was committed to a sanitarium in Battle Creek, Michigan.

One Saturday night, filled with remorse and despair, James wrote farewell notes to his family and friends, stretched out on the bed and waited to die.

But he woke up the next morning . . . and figured he ought to find out why? He heard music. Someone was singing. There was nothing better to do, so he put on his robe and slippers and strolled down the hall. Entering the Chapel . . . he found a seat in the back . . . and listened.

The words of the hymn found a ready place in the aching heart of James Cash. He didn't stay for the sermon. One verse of one hymn was enough. The words of the music had managed a quiet miracle.

Back to the room . . . swiftly. Change clothes. Pack bags. Return to the desk and James checked himself out . . . at fifty-six . . . when most men think only of retiring . . . he started all over again.

And today there are 2,000 stores and more . . . across America and around the world, with his name over the front door. That's right . . . James Cash . . . J. C. . . . Penny.

As wonderful as that story is . . . the undeniable point of it for all of us is the song. The song that turned his life around. That simple miracle message is still good for us today. Please

. . . sing it . . . believe it . . . with all your heart. It is, as the Psalmist wrote, the song that is seen.

> Be not dismayed what e'er betide,
> God will take care of you;
> Beneath His wings of love abide,
> God will take care of you.
>
> God will take care of you,
> Through every day,
> O'er all the way;
> He will take care of you,
> God will take care of you.

36

FATHERS WHO CARED

They are, at best, a strange group of men. Yet one unique bond ties them to each other for as long as America records her history.

One was a poor Irish immigrant who died prematurely, leaving a sister to raise his three young sons.

One was so Dutch that English was not spoken in the home.

Another, Scotch-Irish. A farmer who never quite made it big, except in children . . . he fathered nine.

Another was a trader . . . the best he could do for his wife and 11 children was a one-room house for the entire family.

Two were preachers in small churches.

One was a self-appointed doctor . . . he never earned a real medical degree, but took a course by correspondence, and then went from farm to farm offering his questionable services.

Another was a tanner of hides.

Still another . . . a poor laborer who never lived to see the birth of his youngest son.

Missouri was the home of one. He was a mule trader.

Iowa was the state of another. He was a blacksmith.

Tavern-keeper, trolley car conductor, itinerant salesman, frontiersman . . . none really made a mark in a grand or great way.

Mostly ordinary men, in what could be called at best, small professions. But all of these men made it big in one way . . . and it is this that binds these men of two centuries into one special class.

Each one had a son . . .
            who became a President . . .
                        of the United States.

All of us Dads want to leave a heritage. Something behind that can be easily noted and happily remembered.

Maybe money,
    or fame,
        or power,
            or a good name,
                or a consistent faith,
                    or a lofty reputation,
                        or a committed family man,
                            or a conspicuous achievement.

But perhaps the greatest heritage any child can have is that Daddy really cared. And did something about it.

In Mark, Chapter 9, there is the touching story of the distraught father who wants something from Jesus that no one else can provide. His son is sick . . . very sick . . . absolutely imbalanced. He foams at the mouth and grinds his teeth and falls into convulsions writhing on the ground and going rigid.

Then he falls into fits of deep depression. and loses himself in a swamp of self pity.

Jesus asked the father, "How long has he been like this?"

The father replied, "Since he was a little child. And sometimes he tries to drown himself . . . and he throws himself in a fire trying to burn himself to death. Help, please!"

If you've never lived with a suicidal person, you have no idea of the trauma and tenseness it brings to life. It's an overwhelming combination of helplessness and hopelessness. And it's not hard to see why this father was so desperately moved.

Their conversation continued like this:

Father: If . . .
Jesus: If . . .
Father: If Thou . . .
Jesus: If thou . . .
Father: If Thou canst . . .
Jesus: If thou canst . . .
Father: If Thou canst do . . .
Jesus: If thou canst believe . . .
Father: If Thou canst do anything . . .
Jesus: If thou canst believe, all things are possible.

The father then said . . . with tears . . . "Lord, I believe. Help my unbelief!"

Jesus spoke words of deliverance to the boy, who then went into fit after fit, thrashing around on the ground and screaming loudly, until he got still as a corpse and seemed to be dead.

You know there were those in the crowd who said among themselves, "Now you've gone and done it, Jesus. At least until now this father had a son. Now he has only memories and remains."

But Jesus wasn't through. He reached out His hand and touched the boy . . . who woke as if from a dream, stood on his own two feet, hugged his father in recognition and started on the happy walk back home.

Just because of a father who cared.

And did you know that a man became President of the United States because his son was a poor student? That's right! It all started when Robert tried to get into Harvard back in '59. He had come East from Illinois to take the entrance exams . . . and failed in 15 subjects.

That worried Dad. Like all fathers, he wanted his son to make good grades and get a fine education. so Dad made a fast trip East to bolster Robert's morale and help tutor him in another bid to gain entrance into Harvard.

While he was East Dad was invited to have dinner with a famous editor. That editor was so impressed that he arranged for Dad to give a lecture in New York City.

It was a good speech. His folksy, casual delivery went over big with the New Yorkers. As a result of that one speech, Dad became an overnight sensation.

He was thrust into the national political picture and became a prime candidate for the Republican presidential nomination, which he accepted, and then became President of the United States . . . because he cared about his son, Robert.

The Editor who launched the Presidential career? Horace Greeley.

And the father who became President . . . because his son was a poor student? One of the greatest of all time . . . Abraham Lincoln!

In 1932 the times were hard for most Americans. Charles Darrow was no different. He was an unemployed heating engineer, 42 years old with a wife and family to care for.

Charles started inventing things to keep himself occupied. He came up with some game score pads, jigsaw puzzles and a combination ball and bat beach toy. But none of his ideas proved profitable.

Then Darrow came up with a real estate game as a family diversion for an empty evening. A round piece of oil cloth colored with free paint samples made the playing board. He drew some funny money and cut up shoe boxes for title deeds to property and used colored buttons for playing pieces.

Friends began requesting copies after spending an evening around the oil cloth and soon he was turning out two home-made sets a day. In 1934 he took his idea to Parker Brothers . . . the world's largest producer of games . . . but they turned him down. It seems that Charles broke 52 Golden Rules for successful games.

Darrow returned home to Pennsylvania and had 5000 sets made and by Christmas stores were ordering so many that he was working 14 hours a day to keep up. Parker Brothers watched the sales and in 1935 . . . they reconsidered and changed their rules.

And now Charles Darrow's game is the most popular in the world . . . published in 15 languages. MONOPOLY . . . just because a dad wanted something for his children to do with their evenings.

Let me give you one more . . . Maybe the best I know. Walter had been an all-star basketball player in college. But that had been enough years ago that now he was attending his son's first high school game. With a lot of excitement and crossed fingers for success, Dad sat in the stands, quietly studying the warm-ups and evaluating the abilities of both teams.

Sonny didn't get to start . . . but that was OK with the father. It would allow the ever-present butterflies to calm down in the boy's heart. Big game . . . big crowd. Better to just sit and watch for a while.

Half-way into the second period, with the home team leading by 3, Walt's boy got the call from Coach. This was it! His first real game. But Sonny was so excited, he rushed to center-court, forgetting to take off his warm-up jacket. The bench yelled at him until he realized his mistake. He yanked it off roughly and flung it back toward his team.

The crowd began to snicker when they noticed that his jersey was on backwards. It seemed that everyone was pointing at him and the ref wouldn't let him in the game that way. "Fix the shirt," was his terse command.

Instead of retreating to the cover of his teammates on the bench, Sonny stood at center court and pulled the jersey off over his head, effecting the change in plain view.

Then the crowd stopped giggling and began to laugh in earnest. The sight of a skinny, high school, substitute basket ball player, naked from the waist up was more than they could stand.

"Take it off," yelled one fan. "Take it all off," shouted another . . . this one a female.

Face flushed redder than the shirt, Sonny finally got it all straightened out, nodded to the ref, and the game began again.

Dad sat in a rather stunned silence. Not exactly what he had expected for his son's debut.

The game progressed for 3 more minutes before his son

was really in the action. Dad kept waiting for some burst of brilliance . . . and the moment finally came. A missed shot by a teammate caromed off the rim and into the son's outstretched hands.

An opposing player swatted at it . . . but Sonny spun around protecting the ball. Another player took a whack at it, but Sonny spun again . . . this time the other way.

"Go for the basket," yelled the coach. "Shoot, shoot, shoot," the crowd seemed to roar in unison.

Sonny spun again, dribbled the ball, drove for the basket and stuffed it for the easy two points. Expecting cheers and congratulations, you can be sure he was confused when the crowd groaned and then broke out again in hilarious laughter.

It didn't take Sonny long to figure out that he had dribbled the wrong way . . . stuffed the ball in the wrong basket . . . and scored two points for the wrong team. If ever a boy wanted to crawl into a hole in the floor . . . this was the one. Absolutely embarrassed and overwhelmed by his stupid mistake, Sonny just wanted to die.

And what does a Dad do at that moment. Hide his face in shame? Get up and quietly leave? Or join in the laughter and the boo's . . . hoping no one will recognize him?

Not this father. When would his son ever need him more? So when some fan shouted through his laughter, "Who is that kid?" Walter stood up and said strongly and proudly, "That's my boy!"

Sonny heard it, lifted his head high, and waved at his Dad. Dad held both hands high, clasped over his head in a symbol of triumph and recognition.

Suddenly basketball was not the important issue. What we saw was a father unconditionally loving a boy . . . just because that was his son.

37

STARS AND STRIPES

She was only 25, but the pressures of life had already etched old lines on her girlish face. She had watched and waited for her soldier husband to return, but all that came back was a letter from his commanding officer: "Killed in battle."

So every day became the same. Her hands moving to and fro, tatting lace and sewing hems. But one day was different. A light broke through her shadowed life ... brought by a man who needed her help.

Together they drew and shaped and planned.

Six white bands . . .

seven red stripes . . .

and a corner of blue.

General George Washington suggested stars with six points, but the seamstress was adamant ... no six pointed stars on her flag. Those were British stars, and to them she had lost her husband. Only five pointed stars . . . they were symbols of freedom.

She had her way . . . and Betsy Ross began to make her flags. And as she worked, the light that began in her small

sewing room burst on the world as it touched the sky.
Our flag . . . the symbol of the hopes of man.
. . . the cloth of dreams for freedom,
justice
and opportunity.

Its red stripes are like wounds of struggle . . .
. . . the good in it cannot be had for nothing.

Its white bands are like purest snow . . .
. . . the glory of it cannot be bought or sold.

Its blue field is like a durable peace . . .
. . . rising from the deep dedication of patriots past.

Its stars are like beacons . . .
. . . guiding us through the shoals of adversity.

Like any garden . . . it must be tended.
Like any loved one . . . it must be held.

Lift this flag high and keep its promise bright . . .
for in it lies the best hope for all of us.

If the flag could speak today, what do you think she'd say?
Perhaps . . . some people call me Old Glory, others call me the
Star Spangled Banner, but whatever they call me, I am your
flag, the Flag of the United States of America. Something has
been bothering me, so I though I might talk it over with you .
. . because it's about you and me.

It used to be that people would line up on both sides of the
street to watch the parades that I would lead, proudly waving

242 / E̶ASY D̶OESN'T D̶O I̶T

in the breeze. When the Daddy's saw me coming their hats came off and were held against the left shoulder right over the heart.

And I remember the little boys . . . standing straight as soldiers. Hatless . . . but giving the right salute. And the little sisters . . . not to be outdone . . . saluting the same as their brothers . . . right and over heart.

So what happened? I'm still the same old flag. Oh, I have a few more stars and a lot more scars. Somehow I don't feel as proud as I used to. When I come down your street you just stand there with your hands in your pockets and I may get a short glance before you look away. Then I see the children running around and shouting . . . they don't seem to know who I am. I saw one man take his hat off and then look around. He didn't see anybody else with bared head so he quickly put his hat back on.

Is it wrong to be patriotic anymore? Have all of you forgotten what I stand for and where I've been? Anzio, Guadalcanal, Korea and Vietnam. Take a look at the Memorial Honor Rolls sometime. Those are names of people who went to keep this Republic free . . . one nation under God. When you salute me, you are actually saluting them.

It probably won't be too long until I'll be coming down your street again. So when you see me, stand straight, place your right hand over your heart . . . and I'll salute you by waving back . . . and I'll know that you remembered.

He was only 21. He'd been teaching school for 2 years when the war began. He was a little above average in height, had fair skin, blue eyes and light hair.

He was involved in the Long Island campaign which was just this side of disastrous. We were facing the enemy across the East River not knowing what their plans might be. Fearing surprise more than anything, General Washington wanted someone to sneak over the lines and get information.

Spying is a dirty job and nobody wanted it . . . so Nate volunteered. He was sent through the enemy lines dressed like a Dutch schoolmaster. He got what he went after and was on his way back when the British found the information on him. He admitted he was a spy and they hanged him the next morning.

He wrote some letters home but the British destroyed them. He asked if he might say something? They agreed. He was just a young American who never had time to do anything memorable but die.

He stood there with the noose around his neck and told them his rank . . . Captain. His name . . . Nathan Hale. Then he added, "I only regret that I have but one life to give for my country."

And he showed the world what Americans are made of.

And so it has gone. At Lexington and Valley Forge.
At Gettysburg and the Alamo.
At Flanders Field and Corregidor.
At Normandy and Guadalcanal.
At Pork Chop Hill and Vietnam.

History has been written with blood . . .
. . . before it ever was written with ink.

Listen to the Chaplain at Pearl Harbor,
"Praise the Lord and pass the ammunition!"

Or the Commander on Wake Island saying,
"Don't fire till you see the whites of their eyes!"

Douglas MacArthur leaving the Philippines with the promise,
"I shall return!"

Abraham Lincoln said it for all of us,
"These dead shall not have died in vain!"

On May 17, 1987, an Iraqi rocket struck the U.S.S. Stark, inflicting heavy damage and claiming 36 American lives. At home there was a loud outcry of protest, insisting that the United States Navy immediately withdraw all its forces from the Middle East.

The sailors of the Stark started their own protest which proudly spread from ship to ship. Every seaman had a "T" shirt with a picture of an American flag printed on the chest. . . and underneath were the words:

THESE COLORS DON'T RUN

We had a great line a few years ago in the days of my traveling musical entourage. During a patriotic performance, when one of our young men was introduced as a Souix Indian (he really was) he would look at the audience and say,

"America . . . love it . . . or give it back!"

There are some really dumb people out there, you known?
Very dumb.
Any American who knocks what he's got, that's what he is!

Look at what we have:
A country of unbounded beauty.
Unlimited natural resources.

A judicial system that is the envy of the rest of the world.
Food so plentiful that overeating is a major problem.
A press nobody can dominate.
A ballot box nobody can stuff.
Churches of your choice.
One hundred million jobs.
Freedom to go anywhere we want,
     with the planes, cars and highways to get us there.
Social Security.
Medicare.
Unemployment insurance.
Public schools and plentiful scholarships.
The opportunity to become a millionaire.

O.K., complainer, what's your second choice?

Go!

38

SAY THAT AGAIN . . .

It was hurricane warning season in Florida and we were busy stocking up on all the emergency equipment and supplies that the experts said we needed:

    portable radio (so you can tell how bad things really are),
    flashlights,
    batteries (all sizes . . . your neighbor may need help)
    canned food,
    bottled water,
    wood for the fire place, if you have one (we do)
    charcoal for the grill (that's my idea)
    blankets (color optional)

After we got all the stuff purchased, cataloged and stored, we sat down to wait for the storm. In the interim, it seemed appropriate to have a drill.

How would we find this meaningful material in the dark?
Who would be responsible for which equipment and supply?
If the power was out, where would we assemble in the dark?
How would we exist without a phone (Stephanie's question)?

Does Nintendo work without electricity (Jeremiah's concern)?

Can we wake up on time without the alarm clock (Mommy's worry)?

Does that mean the phone will never ring (Daddy's delight)?

We got past the questions and back into the practical . . . all assignments made and tasks completed. We sat looking at each other for further enlightenment.

> We turned out all the lights (for realism),
> opened a can of soup (for practice),
> lit some wood in the fire place (for fun),
> and switched on the flashlight (for effect).

Wow! No illumination from the flashlight. Jeremiah had it, so Stephanie deemed it proper to grab it away and try it herself. Still didn't work . . . not even with a good shaking. Mommy tried . . . still black as the inside of Jonah's whale.

Daddy to the rescue. A little flashlight psychology was due. Tip it upside down. Turn it over . . . and over . . . and over. Screw the ends on a little tighter. Gently tap it on my leg . . . then hit it harder with my hand . . . then thump it on the floor.

Still dark.

Mommy had the best idea. She had murmured it a few times in her quiet, Quaker voice . . . but I had chosen to avoid the obvious . . . at least at first.

Finally, I had to listen. "What was that you said?" I muttered.

"Check the batteries. Sometimes they can be the problem." Womanly wisdom wins again!

It's not that the batteries were no good . . . they just weren't in there! And who's fault was that? Mine, I guess. No one had been assigned to the loading responsibility . . . and since I was the chief designator . . . my fault.

So stop laughing at me. Even in the dark, that's not very polite.

And then I thought, if Jesus were here in the flesh and teaching today, He would probably say something like,

"You are the light of the world". . . .
BATTERIES NOT INCLUDED!

So you buy a fancy new flashlight. It has a great case, a shiny bulb, and a three-way switch. But on the first dark night, when you really need, it' a dud. Just because you forgot the batteries!

Everything else is just right. How it looks, how it feels, how it moves. Just one thing wrong. It needs external power to become what it is intended to be.

That's life . . . the batteries are never included. They are given . . . from above . . . to those who ask.

And then I thought . . . what else would Jesus say in this contemporary world? How would He use our slogans and metaphors to emphasize His message?

When He was here before, He always spoke in terms and words that everybody could grasp . . . not just some far off, cerebral intelligentsia. When He spoke of "a certain man", as He did in so many of His stories, that always referred to a recognizable person in a contemporary incident.

And when He made analogies, everyone knew exactly what He meant. "I am the door . . . had nothing to do with hinges and latches (as my kids had it pictured). He was alluding to the hole in the wall of a sheep fold. The shepherd would count his sheep as they came in every night, then lay himself across the hole, becoming a "door" to protect the sheep from intruders and, at the same time, keeping them from slipping away.

So what else might Jesus say today besides "batteries not included." You know ... advertising slogans that hit us every day. How about:

"A merry heart doeth good like a medicine"
      ... NO PRESCRIPTION NECESSARY!
 A smile is a silent laugh.
  A grin is a smile to yourself that shows.
   A chuckle is a small laugh, sometimes real,
    sometimes not.
    A snicker is a wicked chuckle.
     A chortle is an old-time, deep-down laugh.
     And a laugh ... is the music of happiness.

"The meek shall inherit the earth"
      ... SOME ASSEMBLY REQUIRED!
 He who fails in his present responsibilities, breaks a
 thread in the pattern, and will find the flaw when he
 may have forgotten the cause.
    Count your obligations,
    Name them one by one;
    And it will surprise you
    What the Lord wants done!

"Walk worthy of the vocation wherewith ye are called."
.. .INSTRUCTION MANUAL AVAILABLE!

It's an atlas,
  a guide book,
    a lamp,
      a mirror,
        a telescope,
          a book of poems,
            a collection of biographies,
              a bundle of letters,
                a hymn book,
                  a compilation of counsel,
                    a dose of medicine,
                      a stimulator of energy,
                        a wardrobe of armor,
                          a sword of honor,
                            and a shield of defense.

"Except ye become as little children . . ."
... SIMPLE ENOUGH FOR A CHILD TO ASSEMBLE

Believe big! More people are humbugged by believing in
  nothing, than by believing too much. When in doubt,
  don't.
Love big! It's worth the risk.
Dream big! Life without a dream is like a hamburger with
  no onions . . . it just doesn't stick with you!

"Rejoice in the Lord always, and again I say, rejoice."
... MAY BE HABIT FORMING

The joyful person
        will accomplish more in the same time,
        will do it better,
        will persevere in it longer,

will develop it farther,
>   than the sad or the sullen.
> Flowers that last have deep roots and bloom late,
>   because things that endure grow slowly.

"Where I am, there ye may be also."
>   .... **RESERVATIONS REQUIRED**

Born once, die twice.
Born twice, die once.
> Christ can forgive any trespass. He can overlook none.
> Too many Church members are starched and ironed . . .
>   but not washed.
> Here's Good News . . . God meets us where we are,
>   because we cannot rise, on our own, to where He
>   would have us be.

"Be filled with the Spirit."
>   ..... **PROVIDE YOUR OWN CONTAINER**

When the ceiling of a man's life is lower than his
possibilities, he needs room for character expansion.
> We are not people who are trying to be better than
the rest, but people who want to become better than they are.
> And always remember . . .
>   God wants spiritual fruit, not religious nuts.

> How about one more?
"Whatsoever He saith unto you, do it!"
>   .... **ONE SIZE FITS ALL**

Two children built a club house in the yard. In childish
letters on the wall were scribbled a list of club rules.
>   **NOBODY ACT BIG**
>   **NOBODY ACT SMALL**
>   **EVERYBODY ACT MEDIUM**

The ground is level at the foot of the Cross.

39

ELECTIVE SERVICE...
MAY I HELP YOU?

Which stranded motorist gets help the soonest... a pregnant woman, a little old lady, a messy hippie, a smartly dressed career woman or a sexy siren?

A Space Coast newspaper decided to find out, and ran a test on Florida's U.S. Route 1 with a 22-year-old actress, Sally Mullins, playing the driver in distress in all five roles.

CAREER WOMAN: Dressed in a double-breasted suit she stood by her "hood-up, broken-down" Pontiac Grand Am, holding a "stop" sign and waited for help. A minute and a half and 62 vehicles later, Bill Leonardi pulled over to offer assistance.

PREGNANT WOMAN: Disguised with about 8 months of padding, she had to wait 2 1/2 minutes while more than 100 cars whizzed past before paramedics Bob Smith and Dorothy Jenning (who had been driving in the opposite direction) made a U-turn in their ambulance to lend Sally a helping hand.

LITTLE OLD LADY: She had to wait nearly 5 minutes and watch 200 vehicles drive by before two people pulled over to help her... 22-year-old college co-ed Glenna Newell and land surveyor Greg Smith, 29.

HIPPIE GIRL: Costumed in faded jeans, a loud floral blouse and wild blonde wig, nobody stopped at all! She stood by her car for more than 15 minutes while over 350 cars, trucks, vans, buses and motorcycles zoomed by. No one even slowed down.

MINI-SKIRTED NYMPH IN NEED: Sally no sooner put up the hood of her car when Ed Kent of West Palm Beach barreled to a stop right behind her. That "damsel in distress" outfit stopped a car in 9 seconds... the fastest of any of them!

That kind of "selective service" gives cause for pause. Remember Jesus' answer to the lawyer's question, "Who is my neighbor?" It was recorded in Luke, chapter 10, when Jesus told the story about an ill-fated traveler. It happened on the 15 mile road between Jerusalem, "head-quarters for God," and Jericho, "the city of curse."

Jesus said there was a "certain man", meaning that this parable is an actual recounting of a real incident that had occurred in the present tense... everybody know about it. Herod's Temple had been completed and unemployment was epidemic. Forty-thousand men had just been laid off and some researchers estimate there were at least 12,000 "thieves" in the hills surrounding Jerusalem. Many of these were good men and upstanding citizens... but they were desperate in

254 / Easy Doesn't Do It

their efforts to provide for their families.

Down this highway through the hills came the traveler. He was confronted by thieves... robbed, beaten and left for dead. Along came two religious leaders... who looked at him... and walked on by. A Samaritan man, outcast by birth and despised in life, stopped to help and offer assistance. "Who was the real neighbor?" Jesus asked. "Figure it out for yourself."

Nearness does not make neighbors... and probably the great question is not "Who is my neighbor? but "Am I neighborly?" There are three fundamental philosophies in this narrative... and they merit scrutiny. Every person has one of them... even us. Especially us! You cannot embrace more than one of these perspectives... but, like it or not, one of them is yours.

First, there is the philosophy of the thief:

WHAT'S YOURS IS MINE . . . I'LL TAKE IT

An old man married a young girl and there marriage was off to a wonderful start. First a legendary honeymoon cruise, then an incredible home, and now the finest friends and the best parties. One night, the groom asked his lovely bride, "If I lost everything, would you still love me?"

Her instant reply, "Sure I'd love you... I'd also miss you!"

That's the philosophy of the thief... what's in this for me? It's a selfish,
>   greedy,
>   heartless,
>   ruthless,
>   egotistical,

        insensitive attitude
           that only and always leads
              to heartache and heartbreak.

It was when I was nine that I found the last big piece of my Mother's special chocolate sponge cake... a regal repast fit for a prince, but not for his little brother. I was stuffing the tasty morsels down as fast as my lips would smack when Mom walked into the kitchen and with great disappointment exclaimed, "Derric, I can't believe you could eat that whole piece of cake without thinking once about your brother.

"Oh, I was thinking about him the whole time I was eating. I kept worrying that he'd come in before I could finish it all!"

'Nuff said about the philosophy of the thief... but how about the two religious leaders who ignored the need and kept on walking? Their fundamental principle is simple:

WHAT'S MINE IS MINE . . . I'LL KEEP IT

Now remember... the Priest is the professional religious person... he's paid to do be pious. His biggest problem was that he left God in the Temple. Job description has nothing to do with godliness.

And the Levite... a servant of the Temple... a minister of religious worship whose faith never got beyond the sanctuary walls and out into real life. And Jesus said, "Shame on you!"

These were men compelled to show mercy to even a lowly beast in trouble... but could find no compassion on or compulsion to help this ill-fated traveler. They folded their robes of righteousness comfortably around themselves and proceeded on the appointed spiritual duties.

Reminiscent of the Church Board addressing the new Pastor, "Of course we want to grow... but do you think you could accomplish that without adding any new people." You know...we love us the way we are.

It is an illusion to think that more comfort means more happiness. Happiness comes of the capacity to feel deeply,

to enjoy simply,
to think freely,
and to be needed.

Interesting that Jesus would use the phrase "by chance" when He spoke of the Priest and Levite coming down the road. The words "by chance" are best defined "a God-planned-opportunity." Always find a way to make the most them... regardless of cost. The highest reward for a man's life-labor is not what he gets from it... but what he becomes by it.

Jesus rebuked them because they were heartless,

self-centered,
withdrawn,
introverted,
compassionless,
and unaware.

On the other hand we have the hero of the story. A Samaritan, a member of a mixture-race... part Jew, part Gentile... and as such, unloved and unwanted by either side of ethnic purists. But here is the man who most effectively demonstrates what Jesus wanted us to be all about:

> giving,
> loving,
> caring,
> and dependable.

His philosophy:

WHAT'S MINE IS YOURS . . . I'LL SHARE IT

A friend of mine in San Diego had just received a new car as a gift from his brother after an enormously successful business transaction. Please understand, we're talking "real car" here... a new Sterling... bright red and very shiny.

He was coming out of a downtown shop when he noticed an awestruck 10 year old boy... jaw down, eyes wide... just standing on the curb admiring the "wheels-of-wealth."

As my friend unlock the door and started to get in, the boy asked, "Hey, Mister... is this your car?"

"It's mine," Ray replied.

"Golly... how much did this thing cost?"

"I don't know... I didn't pay for it."

The boy's eyes brightened and with breathiness he asked, "Did you steal it?"

"No... not hardy. It was a gift. My brother gave it me."

"Yeah? Well... what did he want from you?"

"He didn't want anything from me. He just wanted me to have a new car. He's my brother."

At that the boy's brown furrowed and eyes squinted in disbelief. "You mean... he just gave you this neat, shiny, red car... 'cause he's your brother?"

"That's right," said my friend. "Pretty good brother, huh?"

"I guess so," came the incredulous response. Then the boy added, "Hey, Mister... you know what I wish?"

"Yeah, kid, I know what you wish... but go ahead and tell me anyway."

"Well, Mister... I wish I could be a brother like that!"

You know what you thought he'd say? "I wish I HAD a brother like that!" And do you know why you thought he's say that? Because that's what you would say. And guess who's philosophy that is... the philosophy of the thief who says,

WHAT'S YOURS IS MINE... I WANT IT.

It's no wonder that the world staggers on wounded and confused when those of us who call ourselves by His name run around wanting... instead of giving.

Ray asked the boy if he wanted a ride in the car. At first the kid felt self-conscious, too unsure of his station to get in such an obviously classy-chassis. But Ray insisted on at least a ride around the block.

The boy offered an alternative... could they go past where he lived? It was just down the street and through an alley. Ray agreed and off they went. When they turned down the narrow roadway, the sight of the tenement buildings was unnerving to Ray. But the boy was sitting straight up in the seat, motioning and gesturing grandly to all his buddies who watched him pass with envy.

"Here... here. Please stop for just a minute. I'll be right back," he shouted, jumping from the car and dashing up the stairs to the apartment on the third floor. Ray waited... and then saw the strangest sight. First two feet on the steps... then two dangling feet... attached to a little body... then the rest of the boy. He was carrying his little brother... weak and diseased, but happy.

The 10 year-old sat his 5 year-old sibling on a step next to himself, pointed and said, "See that car. It's red and shiny and brand-new. And someday I'm gonna get you one just like it... 'cause you're my brother!"

The thief says,

WHAT'S YOURS IS MINE, I'LL TAKE IT!

The Priest and Levite say,

WHAT'S MINE IS MINE, I'LL KEEP IT!

The Good Samaritan says,

WHAT'S MINE IS YOURS, I'LL SHARE IT!

So what do you say?

Wisdom is knowing what to do.
Skill is knowing how to do it.
Virtue... is just doing it.